TOUCHSTONE

FAITH

Happiness Is...

Simple Steps to a Life of Joy

A. R. Bernard

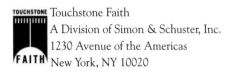 Touchstone Faith
A Division of Simon & Schuster, Inc.
1230 Avenue of the Americas
New York, NY 10020

First Touchstone Faith hardcover edition November 2007

TOUCHSTONE FAITH and colophon are trademarks of Simon & Schuster, Inc.

For information about special discounts for bulk purchases, please contact
Simon & Schuster Special Sales at 1-800-456-6798 or
business@simonandschuster.com.

Designed by Mary Austin Speaker

Manufactured in the United States of America

10 9 8 7 6 5 4 3 2 1

Bernard, A. R. (Alfonso R.)
    Happiness is . . . : simple steps to a life of joy / A. R. Bernard, Sr.
        p. cm.
    "A Touchstone Faith edition."
        1. Happiness—Religious aspects—Christianity. 2. Christian life. I.
    Title.
BV4647.J68B47 2007
248.4—dc22   2007008233

ISBN-13: 978-1-4165-4940-6
ISBN-10:   1-4165-4940-4

Introduction

In the spring of 2004, I read an article in USA *Today* by Kevin Maney entitled "Money Can't Buy Happiness, But Happiness May Buy Money." In it, Mr. Maney summarized some impressive research findings that demonstrate—just like you've heard all your life but may not have really believed—that cash *cannot* buy contentment. The article gave me the idea for a series of sermons on what happiness is—and what it isn't. This book is an extension of those sermons.

Now, I know what you're probably thinking: A big stash of cash may not be able to buy me happiness, but I'd sure like the opportunity to find out for myself! And if that's what you're thinking, then you're no different than billions of people around the globe. We human beings are quick to equate money with happiness, no matter how many times we hear otherwise.

Yet the research shows time and again that money, in and

of itself, simply does not make folks happy. Don't believe me? Well, here's a statistic to think about: Even though the average American's income has tripled (in buying power) since 1956, the number of Americans who say they're happy has stayed about the same, at around 30 percent. So if more money can't purchase contentment for the average American, then you're smart if you *don't* depend upon the "almighty" dollar as your primary tool for becoming a genuinely happy person.

But if money doesn't win happiness, what does? Genuine happiness is a way of mind and a way of life. Happiness results from the way you choose to interpret events and the choices you make as a result of those interpretations. If you choose to view the world in a positive way, if you work hard to achieve positive results, and if you associate with positive people, then you'll increase your odds of being happy (most of the time). But if you refuse to look at the donut and focus instead upon the hole, you can make yourself unhappy (most of the time) even if you've got a bigger bank balance than Bill Gates.

Happiness also depends upon your willingness to be a disciplined person, a person who is focused on doing *what* needs to be done *when* it needs to be done. Happiness depends upon your willingness to lead a purposeful, principled life. And, of course, your happiness depends upon the nature and the quality of your relationship with God.

This book is intended to help you explore happiness: what it means, how to find it, and how to keep it. So during the next fifty-two weeks, try this experiment: Read a chapter each week and spend a few minutes daily thinking about the things you've read. Then apply the lessons you've learned to the ups and downs of everyday life. When you do, you'll discover that happiness isn't a commodity that can be purchased in a store; it's a byproduct of the way you choose to live and the things you choose to think.

The ideas on these pages can—and should—be woven into the fabric of your life. Your life story is being written one day at a time . . . and with God's help, that story can—and will—be a masterpiece.

Happiness Is . . .
Accepting God's Abundance

*I have come that they may have life, and that they may have it
more abundantly.*

—JOHN 10:10 NKJV

God offers us abundance, but He doesn't force it upon
us. He promises that we "might have life" and that we
"might have it more abundantly." And how, precisely
can we claim that abundance? By obeying God and following
His Son, that's how!

When we commit our hearts, our days, and our work to the
One who created us, we experience spiritual abundance. But
when we focus our thoughts and energies, not upon God's will
for our lives, but instead upon our own unending assortments
of earthly needs and desires, we inevitably forfeit the spiritual
abundance that might otherwise be ours.

Today and every day, seek God's will for your life and fol-

low it. Today, turn your worries and your concerns over to your Heavenly Father. Today, seek God's wisdom, follow His commandments, trust His judgment, and honor His Son. And while you're at it, get rid of that critical voice inside your head—the little voice that tells you you're never quite good enough. When you do these things, you'll receive God's abundance . . . and you'll be happy.

Great Ideas About Abundance

God loves you and wants you to experience peace and life—abundant and eternal.

—BILLY GRAHAM

We honor God by asking for great things when they are a part of His promise. We dishonor Him and cheat ourselves when we ask for molehills where He has promised mountains.

—VANCE HAVNER

Greatness occurs when your children love you, when your critics respect you, and when you have peace of mind.

—QUINCY JONES

God is the giver and we are the receivers; and it is not to those who do great things, but to those who "receive abundance of grace, and of the gift of righteousness," that richest promises are made.

—HANNAH WHITALL SMITH

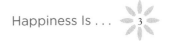

You can have it all. You just can't have it all at once.

—OPRAH WINFREY

More from God's Word

And God will generously provide all you need. Then you will always have everything you need and plenty left over to share with others.

—2 CORINTHIANS 9:8 NLT

Ask and it will be given to you; seek and you will find; knock and the door will be opened to you. For everyone who asks receives; he who seeks finds; and to him who knocks, the door will be opened.

—MATTHEW 7:7-8 NIV

A Simple Step

Abundance and obedience go hand in hand. Obey God first and expect to receive His abundance second, not vice versa.

Your Thoughts

Happiness Is . . .
Learning to Accept the Past

*One thing I do, forgetting those things which are behind and
reaching forward to those things which are ahead, I press toward
the goal for the prize of the upward call of God in Christ Jesus.*

—PHILIPPIANS 3:13–14 NKJV

You'll never find lasting happiness unless you learn to
make peace with the past. You'll never be contented
until you learn how to look back upon your own experiences—both your victories and your disappointments—with a
sense of acceptance and thanksgiving. In short, you must learn
how to interpret your own personal history in a positive way.

Have you made peace with your past? If so, congratulations. But if you're still mired in the quicksand of regret, it's
time to plan your escape. How can you do so? By accepting
what has been and by trusting God for what will be.

Because you're only human, you may be slow to forget

yesterday's setbacks; if so, you are not alone. But if you sincerely want to find enduring happiness, you must find ways to entrust the past to God and then move on with your life.

If you have not yet made peace with the past, this is the day to declare an end to all hostilities. When you do, you can then direct your thoughts to the exciting future that God has in store for you.

Great Ideas About Acceptance

Have courage for the great sorrows of life and patience for the small ones, and when you have laboriously accomplished your daily task, go to sleep in peace. God is awake.

—VICTOR HUGO

Acceptance says: True, this is my situation at the moment. I'll look unblinkingly at the reality of it. But I'll also open my hands to accept willingly whatever a loving Father sends me.

—CATHERINE MARSHALL

We must meet our disappointments, our thwartings, our persecutions, our malicious enemies, our provoking friends, our trials and temptations of every sort, with an active and experimental attitude of surrender and trust. We must spread our wings and "mount up" to the "heavenly places in Christ" above them all, where they will lose their power to harm or distress us.

—HANNAH WHITALL SMITH

Surrender to the Lord is not a tremendous sacrifice, not an agonizing performance. It is the most sensible thing you can do.

—CORRIE TEN BOOM

We must accept finite disappointment, but we must never lose infinite hope.

—MARTIN LUTHER KING JR.

Don't let your future be held captive by your past.

—A. R. BERNARD

More from God's Word

Give in to God, come to terms with him and everything will turn out just fine.

—JOB 22:21 MSG

Do not remember the past events, pay no attention to things of old. Look, I am about to do something new; even now it is coming. Do you not see it? Indeed, I will make a way in the wilderness, rivers in the desert.

—ISAIAH 43:18-19 HCSB

A Simple Step

Maybe you think your past has been negative. But God doesn't build anything on a negative. He always builds on a positive. So don't focus on the negatives in your past . . . focus on the positives.

Your Thoughts

3

Happiness Is . . .
Learning How to Endure Hardships with Patience and Trust

*Consider it pure joy, my brothers, whenever you face trials of
many kinds, because you know that the testing of your faith
develops perseverance. Perseverance must finish its work so that
you may be mature and complete, not lacking anything.*

—JAMES 1:2–4 NIV

Happiness is learning how to deal with the inevitable
disappointments of life. When we are troubled, God
stands ready and willing to protect us. Our responsibility, of course, is to ask Him for protection. When we call
upon Him in heartfelt prayer, He will answer—in His own time
and in accordance with His own perfect plan.

Life is often challenging, but we must not be afraid. God
loves us, and He will protect us. In times of hardship, He will

comfort us; in times of sorrow, He will dry our tears. When we are troubled or weak or sorrowful, God is always with us. We must build our lives on the rock that cannot be shaken: We must trust in God. And then, we must get on with the hard work of tackling our problems . . . because if we don't, who will? Or should?

Great Ideas About Adversity

Often the trials we mourn are really gateways into the good things we long for.

—HANNAH WHITALL SMITH

Never let your head hang down. Never give up and sit down and grieve. Find another way.

—LEROY "SATCHEL" PAIGE

Recently I've been learning that life comes down to this: God is in everything. Regardless of what difficulties I am experiencing at the moment, or what things aren't as I would like them to be, I look at the circumstances and say, "Lord, what are you trying to teach me?"

—CATHERINE MARSHALL

The ultimate measure of a man is not where he stands in moments of comfort and convenience, but where he stands at times of challenge and controversy.

—MARTIN LUTHER KING JR.

The size of your burden is never as important as the way you carry it.

—LENA HORNE

Hidden behind every difficulty is at least one opportunity, and maybe more.

—A. R. BERNARD

More from God's Word

We also have joy with our troubles, because we know that these troubles produce patience. And patience produces character, and character produces hope.

—ROMANS 5:3–4 NCV

The Lord lifts up those who are weighed down. The Lord loves the godly.

—PSALM 146:8 NLT

A Simple Step

When tough times arrive, you should work as if everything depended on you and pray as if everything depended on God.

Your Thoughts

4

Happiness Is . . .
Learning to Control Negative Emotions

My dear brothers and sisters, always be willing to listen and slow to speak. Do not become angry easily, because anger will not help you live the right kind of life God wants.

—JAMES 1:19–20 NCV

Happiness is freedom from all those pesky negative emotions: emotions such as worry, low self-esteem, envy, greed, resentment, prejudice, hatred, and discouragement, for starters. Of course, the list of self-defeating emotions doesn't stop there, but you get the idea.

So what can you do to deliver yourself from the evils of these misdirected thoughts? Well, you can start by slowing down, stepping back, and thinking carefully about the things you've been thinking . . . and why. And while you're thinking things through, you'll want to recount your blessings, "re-

thank" your Creator, and review who—or what—may be pulling your emotional strings.

Human emotions are highly variable, decidedly unpredictable, and often unreliable. Our emotions are like the weather, only sometimes far more fickle. So we must learn to rein in the negative thoughts that might otherwise derail our days and our lives. In short, we must learn to reject negative emotions and the negative people who spread them around.

Some folks are just plain gloomy . . . about everything. These unfortunate people have nothing good to say about anybody, and they'll encourage you to join in their misery. You can choose to join in if you want, but you're better off if you don't. In fact, if you want to remain healthy and happy, you'll work hard to steer clear of these negativity specialists. That's why I have a little sign in a black frame sitting on my desk. It was given to me by one of my parishioners we affectionately call the Tambourine Lady. It faces the door in clear sight of whoever walks in. It says, "Warning! Negative Energy–Free Area. Please think positive before entering."

Who's pulling your emotional strings? Are you allowing highly emotional people or highly charged situations to dictate your moods, or are you wiser than that?

Sometime during the coming days, you may encounter a tough situation or a difficult person. And as a result, you may be gripped by a strong negative emotion. Distrust it. Rein it in. Test it. And turn it over to God.

Your emotions will inevitably change; God will not. So trust

Him completely. When you do, you'll be surprised at how quickly those negative feelings can evaporate into thin air.

Great Ideas About Bitterness

We plant seeds that will flower as results in our lives, so best to remove the weeds of anger, avarice, envy and doubt, that peace and abundance may manifest for all.

—DOROTHY DAY

When we get rid of inner conflicts and wrong attitudes toward life, we will almost automatically burst into joy.

—E. STANLEY JONES

Do not build up obstacles in your imagination. Difficulties must be studied and dealt with, but they must not be magnified by fear.

—NORMAN VINCENT PEALE

Winners see an answer for every problem; losers see a problem in every answer.

—BARBARA JOHNSON

Don't bring negatives to my door.

—MAYA ANGELOU

Bitterness is the acid of the soul, burning away your hopes and dreams.

—A. R. BERNARD

More from God's Word

Do not be afraid or discouraged, for the Lord will personally go ahead of you. He will be with you; he will neither fail you nor abandon you.

—DEUTERONOMY 31:8 NLT

But as for you, be strong; don't be discouraged, for your work has a reward.

—2 CHRONICLES 15:7 HCSB

A Simple Step

Negative thinking breeds more negative thinking, so nip negativity in the bud, starting today and continuing every day of your life. Remember, the cross is a positive sign +.

Your Thoughts

5

Happiness Is . . .
Living in Accordance with Your Beliefs

Do what God's teaching says; when you only listen and do nothing, you are fooling yourselves.

—JAMES 1:22 NCV

L ife is a series of choices. Each day, we make countless decisions that can bring us closer to God . . . or not. When we live according to God's commandments, we earn for ourselves the abundance and peace that He intends for our lives. But, when we turn our backs upon God by ignoring Him—or by disobeying Him—we bring needless pain and suffering upon ourselves and our families.

Do you want God's peace and His blessings? Then obey Him. When you're faced with a difficult choice or a powerful temptation, seek God's counsel and trust the counsel He gives. Invite God into your heart and live according to His commandments.

And when God speaks to you through that little quiet voice that He has placed in your heart, listen. When you do, you will be blessed today, and tomorrow, and forever. And you'll discover that happiness means living in accordance with your beliefs. No exceptions.

Great Ideas About Behavior

The time is always right to do what is right.

—MARTIN LUTHER KING JR.

If you want to be respected for your actions, then your behavior must be above reproach.

—ROSA PARKS

Don't worry about what you do not understand. Worry about what you do understand in the Bible but do not live by.

—CORRIE TEN BOOM

When you discover the Christian way, you discover your own way as a person.

—E. STANLEY JONES

Christianity says we were created by a righteous God to flourish and be exhilarated in a righteous environment. God has "wired" us in such a way that the more righteous we are, the more we'll actually enjoy life.

—BILL HYBELS

Peace and prosperity are the natural results of righteous living.

—A. R. BERNARD

More from God's Word

Don't be deceived: God is not mocked. For whatever a man sows he will also reap, because the one who sows to his flesh will reap corruption from the flesh, but the one who sows to the Spirit will reap eternal life from the Spirit.

—GALATIANS 6:7-8 HCSB

Therefore, get your minds ready for action, being self-disciplined, and set your hope completely on the grace to be brought to you at the revelation of Jesus Christ. As obedient children, do not be conformed to the desires of your former ignorance but, as the One who called you is holy, you also are to be holy in all your conduct.

—1 PETER 1:13-15 HCSB

A Simple Step

Face it: Talking about your beliefs is easy. But making your actions match your words is much harder! Why? Because you are a normal human being, and that means that you can be tempted by stuff and by people. Nevertheless, if you really want to be honest with yourself, then you must make your actions match your beliefs. Period.

Your Thoughts

6

Happiness Is . . .
Counting Your Blessings

*For surely, O Lord, you bless the righteous; you surround them
with your favor as with a shield.*

—PSALM 5:12 NIV

If you sat down and began counting your blessings, how long
would it take? A very, very long time! Your blessings include
life, freedom, family, friends, talents, and possessions, for
starters. But, your greatest blessing—a gift that is yours for the
asking—is God's gift of salvation through Christ Jesus.

Are you a thankful believer who takes time each day to
take a partial inventory of the gifts that God has given you?
Hopefully, you are that kind of Christian. After all, God's Word
makes it clear: A happy heart is a thankful heart.

We honor God, in part, by the genuine gratitude we feel
in our hearts for the blessings He has bestowed upon us. Yet
even the most saintly among us must endure periods of fear,

doubt, and regret. Why? Because we are imperfect human beings who are incapable of perfect gratitude. Still, even on life's darker days, we must seek to cleanse our hearts of negative emotions and fill them instead with praise, with love, with hope, and with thanksgiving. To do otherwise is to be unfair to ourselves, to our loved ones, and to our God.

Today, begin making a list of your blessings. You most certainly will not be able to make a complete list, but take a few moments and jot down as many blessings as you can. Then give thanks to the Giver of all good things: God. His love for you is eternal, as are His gifts. And it's never too soon—or too late—to offer Him thanks.

Great Ideas About Blessings

Blessings we enjoy daily; and for most of them, because they are so common, most men forget to pay their praises.

—IZAAK WALTON

There is no secret that can separate you from God's love; there is no secret that can separate you from His blessings; there is no secret that is worth keeping from His grace.

—SERITA ANN JAKES

God is more anxious to bestow His blessings on us than we are to receive them.

—ST. AUGUSTINE

God blesses us in spite of our lives and not because of our lives.

—MAX LUCADO

Think of the blessings we so easily take for granted: Life itself; preservation from danger; every bit of health we enjoy; every hour of liberty; the ability to see, to hear, to speak, to think, and to imagine all this comes from the hand of God.

—BILLY GRAHAM

More from God's Word

The Lord is merciful and compassionate, slow to get angry and filled with unfailing love. The Lord is good to everyone. He showers compassion on all His creation.

—PSALM 145:8–9 NLT

The Lord bless you and keep you; The Lord make His face shine upon you, And be gracious to you.

—NUMBERS 6:24–25 NKJV

A Simple Step

Carve out time to thank God for His blessings. Take time out of every day (not just on Sundays) to praise God and thank Him for His gifts. Live life with an attitude of gratitude.

Your Thoughts

7

Happiness Is . . .
Looking on the Sunny Side

A cheerful heart has a continual feast.

—PROVERBS 15:15 HCSB

C heerfulness is a gift that we give to others and to ourselves. And, as believers who have been saved by a risen
Christ, why shouldn't we be cheerful? The answer, of
course, is that we have every reason to honor our Savior with
joy in our hearts, smiles on our faces, and words of celebration
on our lips.

How cheerful are you? Do you spend most of your day celebrating your life or complaining about it? If you're a big-time
celebrator, keep celebrating. But if you've established the bad
habit of looking at the hole instead of the donut, it's time to
correct your spiritual vision.

Pessimism and doubt are two of the most important tools
that the devil uses to achieve his objectives. Your challenge, of

course, is to ensure that the devil cannot use these tools on you. So today make sure to celebrate the life that God has given you. Your Creator has blessed you beyond measure. Honor Him with your prayers, your words, your deeds, and your joy.

Great Ideas About Cheerfulness

A cloudy day is no match for a sunny disposition.

—WILLIAM ARTHUR WARD

The people whom I have seen succeed best in life have always been cheerful and hopeful people who went about their business with a smile on their faces.

—CHARLES KINGSLEY

God is good, and heaven is forever. And if those two facts don't cheer you up, nothing will.

—MARIE T. FREEMAN

We may run, walk, stumble, drive, or fly, but let us never lose sight of the reason for the journey, or miss a chance to see a rainbow on the way.

—GLORIA GAITHER

Christ can put a spring in your step and a thrill in your heart. Optimism and cheerfulness are products of knowing Christ.

—BILLY GRAHAM

More from God's Word

Be cheerful. Keep things in good repair. Keep your spirits up. Think in harmony. Be agreeable. Do all that, and the God of love and peace will be with you for sure.

—2 CORINTHIANS 13:11 MSG

Do everything readily and cheerfully—no bickering, no second-guessing allowed! Go out into the world uncorrupted, a breath of fresh air in this squalid and polluted society. Provide people with a glimpse of good living and of the living God. Carry the light-giving Message into the night.

—PHILIPPIANS 2:14–15 MSG

A Simple Step

Do you need a little cheering up? Cheer up somebody else. When you brighten somebody else's day, you brighten up your own day, too.

Your Thoughts

8

Happiness Is . . . Listening to Your Conscience

Now the goal of our instruction is love from a pure heart, a good conscience, and a sincere faith.

—I TIMOTHY 1:5 HCSB

Do you want to be happy? Then you must live in accordance with your beliefs. Why? Because if you believe one thing but do something else, your conscience simply won't allow you to enjoy the peace and contentment that can—and should—be yours.

God gave you a conscience for a very good reason: to use it. But, as Billy Graham correctly observed, "Most of us follow our conscience as we follow a wheelbarrow. We push it in front of us in the direction we want to go." To do so, of course, is a very big mistake. Yet all of us, on occasion, have failed to listen to the voice that God planted in our hearts, and all of us have suffered the consequences.

Is your life a picture book of your creed? Are your actions consistent with your personal code? And are you willing to practice the philosophy that you preach? If so, you're both wise and blessed. But if you're doing things that don't meet with approval of the person you see in the mirror, it's time to slow down, to step back, and to think about how your conduct is shaping your character. If you profess to be a Christian but behave yourself as if you were not, you're living in denial, which, by the way, is a very unhappy place to live.

So today make certain that your actions are guided by God's Word and by the conscience that He has placed in your heart. Don't treat your faith as if it were separate from everyday life—instead, weave your beliefs into the very fabric of your day. When you do, God will honor your good works, your good works will honor God, and everybody will be happy.

Great Ideas About Conscience

Reason often makes mistakes, but conscience never does.

—JOSH BILLINGS

Your conscience is your alarm system. It's your protection.

—CHARLES STANLEY

It is neither safe nor prudent to do anything against conscience.

—MARTIN LUTHER

God desires that we become spiritually healthy enough through faith to have a conscience that rightly interprets the work of the Holy Spirit.

—BETH MOORE

A good conscience is a continual feast.

—FRANCIS BACON

More from God's Word

Blessed are those who have a tender conscience, but the stubborn are headed for serious trouble.

—PROVERBS 28:14 NLT

Behold, the kingdom of God is within you.

—LUKE 17:21 KJV

A Simple Step

The more important the decision . . . the more carefully you should listen to your conscience.

Your Thoughts

9

Happiness Is . . .
A Choice

I am not telling you this because I need anything. I have learned
to be satisfied with the things I have and with everything that
happens. I know how to live when I am poor, and I know how to
live when I have plenty. I have learned the secret of being happy
at any time in everything that happens.

—PHILIPPIANS 4:11–12 NCV

appiness is a choice—it depends on how you interpret life. To be happy, you must learn to interpret the
world and its events in a positive fashion. This means
that you begin programming yourself to see the good in everything—no matter what happens, no matter what goes down.
Then, when you find the good in every situation, you take that
good, and you build upon it.

It's amazing how many people, especially those who portray themselves as "victims," conclude that the lives they're

experiencing have been chosen for them. But they're mistaken. In truth, their lives—all of our lives—are composed of our choices . . . and we become servants to the choices we make.

Every life, including yours, is a tapestry of choices. And the quality of your life depends, to a surprising extent, on the quality of the choices you make.

Would you like to enjoy a life of abundance and significance? If so, you must make choices that are pleasing to God.

From the instant you wake up in the morning until the moment you nod off to sleep at night, you make lots of decisions: decisions about the things you do, decisions about the words you speak, and decisions about the thoughts you choose to think. Today and every day, it's up to you (and only you) to make wise choices, choices that enhance your life and build a stronger relationship with the Creator. After all, He deserves your best . . . and so do you.

Great Ideas About Contentment

The life of strain is difficult. The life of inner peace—a life that comes from a positive attitude—is the easiest type of existence.

—NORMAN VINCENT PEALE

If God chooses to remain silent, faith is content.

—RUTH BELL GRAHAM

Contentment is something we learn by adhering to the basics—cultivating a growing relationship with Jesus Christ, living daily, and knowing that Christ strengthens us for every challenge.

—CHARLES STANLEY

The happiness which brings enduring worth to life is not the superficial happiness that is dependent on circumstances. It is the happiness and contentment that fills the soul even in the midst of the most distressing of circumstances and most bitter environment.

—BILLY GRAHAM

True contentment comes from godliness in the heart, not from wealth in the hand.

—WARREN WIERSBE

If you want a better life, make better choices.

—A. R. BERNARD

More from God's Word

But godliness with contentment is great gain. For we brought nothing into the world, and we can take nothing out of it. But if we have food and clothing, we will be content with that.

—1 TIMOTHY 6:6–8 NIV

A tranquil heart is life to the body, but jealousy is rottenness to the bones.

—PROVERBS 14:30 HCSB

A Simple Step

Every major failure in life—whether it's related to love, health,
money, or anything else—every major failure is simply the result of
a lot of little failures along the way that were never attended to.
Little failures add up if you let them . . . so don't let them.

Your Thoughts

10

Happiness Is . . .
Freedom from Fear

Do not be afraid or discouraged. For the LORD your God is
with you wherever you go.

—JOSHUA 1:9 NLT

Happiness is freedom from fear—but sometimes, it's hard
to live courageously. Why? Because we live in a fear-
based world, a world where bad news travels at light
speed and good news doesn't. These are troubled times, times
when we have legitimate fears for the future of our nation, our
world, and our families. But as Christians, we have every reason
to live courageously. After all, the ultimate battle has already
been fought and won on that faraway cross at Calvary.

Perhaps you, like countless other believers, have found
your courage tested by the anxieties and fears that are an inevitable part of life in the twenty-first century. If so, God wants to
have a little talk with you. The next time you find your cour-

age tested to the limit, God wants to remind you that He is not just near; He is here.

Your Heavenly Father is your Protector and your Deliverer. Call upon Him whenever you need Him . . . and be comforted. Whatever your challenge, whatever your trouble, God can handle it. And will.

Great Ideas About Courage

God did away with all my fear.

—ROSA PARKS

There comes a time when we simply have to face the challenges in our lives and stop backing down.

—JOHN ELDREDGE

Just as courage is faith in good, so discouragement is faith in evil, and, while courage opens the door to good, discouragement opens it to evil.

—HANNAH WHITALL SMITH

Fear brings out the worst in everybody.

—MAYA ANGELOU

I have a lot of things to prove to myself. One is that I can live my life fearlessly.

—OPRAH WINFREY

F.E.A.R. = False Evidence that Appears Real.

More from God's Word

When Jesus heard it, He answered him, "Don't be afraid. Only believe."

—LUKE 8:50 HCSB

But He said to them, "Why are you fearful, you of little faith?" Then He got up and rebuked the winds and the sea. And there was a great calm.

—MATTHEW 8:26 HCSB

For God hath not given us the spirit of fear; but of power, and of love, and of a sound mind.

—2 TIMOTHY 1:7 KJV

A Simple Step

Are you feeling anxious or fearful? If so, trust God to handle those problems that are simply too big for you to solve. Entrust the future—and your future—to God. Then, spend a few minutes thinking about specific steps you can take to confront—and conquer—your fears.

Your Thoughts

11

Happiness Is . . .
A Result of Discipline

Therefore, get your minds ready for action, being self-disciplined, and set your hope completely on the grace to be brought to you at the revelation of Jesus Christ.

— I PETER I:I3 HCSB

Happiness is a way of life, a way of summoning the discipline that inevitably leads to success and accomplishment. So if you really want to be happy, you'll need to be a disciplined person, no exceptions.

God's Word reminds us again and again that our Creator expects us to lead disciplined lives. God doesn't reward laziness, misbehavior, or apathy. To the contrary, He expects believers to behave with dignity and discipline.

We live in a world in which leisure is glorified and indifference is often glamourized. But God has other plans. He did not create us for lives of mediocrity; He created us for far greater things.

Life's greatest rewards seldom fall into our laps; to the contrary, our greatest accomplishments usually require lots of work, which is perfectly fine with God. After all, He knows that we're up to the task, and He has big plans for us. The rest, of course, is up to us.

Great Ideas About Discipline

Self-discipline, as a virtue or an acquired asset, can be invaluable to anyone.

—DUKE ELLINGTON

God cannot build character without our cooperation. If we resist Him, then He chastens us into submission. But, if we submit to Him, then He can accomplish His work. He is not satisfied with a halfway job. God wants a perfect work; He wants a finished product that is mature and complete.

—WARREN WIERSBE

As we seek to become disciples of Jesus Christ, we should never forget that the word *disciple* is directly related to the word *discipline*. To be a disciple of the Lord Jesus Christ is to know His discipline.

—DENNIS SWANBERG

Champions aren't made in gyms. Champions are made from something they have deep inside them—a desire, a dream, a

vision. . . . They have to have the skill, and the will. But the will must be stronger than the skill.

—MUHAMMAD ALI

Don't feel entitled to anything you didn't sweat and struggle for.

—MARIAN WRIGHT EDELMAN

Discipline is the bridge between thought and accomplishment.

—JIM ROHN

More from God's Word

God hasn't invited us into a disorderly, unkempt life but into something holy and beautiful—as beautiful on the inside as the outside.

—1 THESSALONIANS 4:7 MSG

Discipline yourself for the purpose of godliness.

—1 TIMOTHY 4:7 NASB

A Simple Step

You need a library. Pick and choose your books wisely. Make sure they're going to build you up. Be sure that your library makes you stronger, healthier, and wiser.

Your Thoughts

12

Happiness Is . . .
Losing the Loser's Limp by Overcoming Excuses

Don't be fooled by those who try to excuse these sins, for the terrible anger of God comes upon all those who disobey him.

EPHESIANS 5:6 NLT

Happiness is growing up. And you will never grow up—you will never mature into a fully functioning adult—until you're willing to accept responsibility for your thoughts, your motives, your words, and your actions. You must toss away all the excuses for failure, and you must stop playing the blame game. In other words, you must rid yourself of the "loser's limp"—blaming your poor performance on imagined injuries—and you must face up to your mistakes.

All too often we're encouraged to proclaim ourselves "victims"; it's a handy way to avoid taking responsibility for our actions. So we make excuses, excuses, and more excuses—with predictably poor results.

We live in a world where excuses are everywhere. And it's precisely because excuses are so numerous that they are also so ineffective. When we hear the words, "I'm sorry but . . . ," most of us already know exactly what is to follow—the big excuse. The dog ate the homework. Traffic was terrible. It's the company's fault. The boss is to blame. The equipment is broken. We're out of that. And so forth and so on.

Because we humans are such creative excuse makers, all of the really good excuses have already been taken. In fact, the high-quality excuses have been used, reused, overused, and abused. That's why excuses don't work—we've heard them all before.

So, if you're wasting your time trying to portray yourself as a victim, or if you're trying to concoct a new and improved excuse, don't bother. Excuses don't work, and while you're inventing them, neither do you. So get rid of the loser's limp. Today!

Great Ideas About Excuses

One thing I don't believe in: excuses.

—KARL MALONE

Hold yourself responsible for a higher standard than anybody else expects of you. Never excuse yourself. Never pity yourself.

Be a hard master to yourself—and be lenient to everybody else.

—HENRY WARD BEECHER

Replace your excuses with fresh determination.

—CHARLES SWINDOLL

Making up a string of excuses is usually harder than doing the work.

—MARIE T. FREEMAN

Excuses are no good. Your friends don't need them, and your enemies won't believe them.

—JAKE GAITHER

If you're not taking responsibility for your own failures, good reasons often make poor excuses.

—A. R. BERNARD

More from God's Word

Do not lack diligence; be fervent in spirit; serve the Lord.

—ROMANS 12:11 HCSB

Observe people who are good at their work—skilled workers are always in demand and admired; they don't take a backseat to anyone.

—PROVERBS 22:29 MSG

A Simple Step

Today, think of something important that you've been putting off.
Then think of the excuses you've used to avoid that responsibility.
Finally, ask yourself what you can do today to finish the work
you've been avoiding.

Your Thoughts

13

Happiness Is . . .
Learning to Forgive Others
(and Yourself)

All bitterness, anger and wrath, insult and slander must be
removed from you, along with all wickedness. And be kind and
compassionate to one another, forgiving one another, just as God
also forgave you in Christ.

—EPHESIANS 4:31–32 HCSB

It's a fact: If you can't forgive, you're not free . . . and you're not happy.

Are you mired in the quicksand of bitterness or regret? If so, you are not only disobeying God's Word, you are also wasting your time.

Being imperfect human beings, most of us are quick to anger, quick to blame, slow to forgive, and even slower to forget. Yet as Christians, we are commanded to forgive others, just as we, too, have been forgiven.

If there exists even one person—alive or dead—against whom you hold bitter feelings, it's time to forgive. Or if you are angry with yourself for some past mistake or shortcoming, it's finally time to forgive yourself and move on. Hatred, bitterness, and regret are not part of God's plan for your life. Forgiveness is.

Great Ideas About Forgiveness

Learning how to forgive and forget is one of the secrets of a happy Christian life.

—WARREN WIERSBE

Forgiveness is nothing compared to forgetting.

—BESSIE DELANY

Our relationships with other people are of primary importance to God. Because God is love, He cannot tolerate any unforgiveness or hardness in us toward any individual.

—CATHERINE MARSHALL

Forgiveness is not an emotion. Forgiveness is an act of the will, and the will can function regardless of the temperature of the heart.

—CORRIE TEN BOOM

We must develop and maintain the capacity to forgive.

—MARTIN LUTHER KING JR.

Whatever offense you fail to forgive, you attach to yourself for the rest of your life.

—A. R. BERNARD

More from God's Word

Be even-tempered, content with second place, quick to forgive an offense. Forgive as quickly and completely as the Master forgave you. And regardless of what else you put on, wear love. It's your basic, all-purpose garment. Never be without it.

—COLOSSIANS 3:13-14 MSG

Whenever you stand praying, forgive, if you have anything against anyone, so that your Father who is in heaven will also forgive you your transgressions.

—MARK 11:25 NASB

A Simple Step

What if it's really hard to forgive somebody? If forgiveness were easy, everybody would be doing it—but it's not always easy to forgive and forget. If you simply can't seem to forgive somebody, pray about it . . . and keep praying about it . . . until God helps you do the right thing.

Your Thoughts

14

Happiness Is . . .
Having Happy Friends

A friend loves you all the time, and a brother helps in time of trouble.

—PROVERBS 17:17 NCV

D o you want to be happy? Then make sure that you pick out friends who are happy, too. Why? Because happiness, like all human emotions, is contagious.

When you associate with positive people, you'll feel better about yourself and your world—but when you hang around with negative people, you won't. So if you really want to feel better about yourself and your circumstances, you'll need to think carefully about the friends you choose to make—and the ones you choose to keep.

If you're really serious about being an optimistic, upbeat, hope-filled person, make sure that your friends feel the same way. Because if you become involved with upbeat people, you'll tend to be an upbeat person, too. But if you hang out with the

critics, the cynics, and the naysayers, you'll find yourself becoming a cynic, too. And life is far too short for that.

Great Ideas About Friendship

A friend is a present you give yourself.

—ROBERT LOUIS STEVENSON

The glory of friendship is not the outstretched hand, or the kindly smile, or the joy of companionship. It is the spiritual inspiration that comes to one when he discovers that someone else believes in him and is willing to trust him with his friendship.

—CORRIE TEN BOOM

In friendship, God opens your eyes to the glories of Himself.

—JONI EARECKSON TADA

A friend gathers all the pieces and gives them back in the right order.

—TONI MORRISON

To get the full value of joy, you must have someone to divide it with.

—MARK TWAIN

A friend is a person who knows all about you but loves you anyway.

—A. R. BERNARD

More from God's Word

Beloved, if God so loved us, we also ought to love one another.

—1 JOHN 4:11 NKJV

This is my command: Love one another the way I loved you. This is the very best way to love. Put your life on the line for your friends.

—JOHN 15:12–13 MSG

A Simple Step

Your friends will have a major impact on your self-image. That's an important reason (but not the only reason) to select your friends carefully.

Your Thoughts

15

Happiness Is . . .
Sow Generously

Remember this: The person who sows sparingly will also reap sparingly, and the person who sows generously will also reap generously.

—2 CORINTHIANS 9:6 HCSB

It's not too complicated: Input determines output. What you sow is what you reap. If you want to be happy, sow generously; if not, sow sparsely.

The thread of generosity is woven—completely and inextricably—into the very fabric of Christ's teachings. As He sent His disciples out to heal the sick and spread God's message of salvation, Jesus offered this guiding principle: "Freely you have received, freely give" (Matthew 10:8 NIV). The principle still applies. If we are to be disciples of Christ, we must give freely of our time, our possessions, and our love.

In 2 Corinthians 9, Paul reminds us that when we sow the seeds of generosity, we reap bountiful rewards in accordance with God's plan for our lives. Thus, we are instructed to give cheerfully and without reservation: "But this I say, He which soweth sparingly shall reap also sparingly; and he which soweth bountifully shall reap also bountifully. Every man according as he purposeth in his heart, so let him give; not grudgingly, or of necessity: for God loveth a cheerful giver" (vv. 6–7 KJV). Today, make this pledge and keep it: Be a cheerful, generous, courageous giver. The world needs your help, and you need the spiritual rewards that will be yours when you give it.

Great Ideas About Generosity

Success has nothing to do with what you gain in life or accomplish for yourself. It's what you do for others.

—DANNY THOMAS

Find out how much God has given you and from it take what you need; the remainder is needed by others.

—ST. AUGUSTINE

To show great love for God and our neighbor, we need not do great things. It is how much love we put in the doing that makes our offering something beautiful for God.

—MOTHER TERESA

Service is the rent you pay for room on this earth.

—SHIRLEY CHISHOLM

The happiest people are those who do the most for others.

—BOOKER T. WASHINGTON

More from God's Word

He did it with all his heart. So he prospered.

—2 CHRONICLES 31:21 NKJV

Be strong and brave, and do the work. Don't be afraid or discouraged, because the Lord God, my God, is with you. He will not fail you or leave you.

—1 CHRONICLES 28:20 NCV

Then, when Job prayed for his friends, the Lord restored his wealth and happiness! In fact, the Lord gave him twice as much as before!

—JOB 42:10 TLB

A Simple Step

There is a direct relationship between generosity and happiness—the more you give to others, the more joy you will experience for yourself.

Your Thoughts

16

Happiness Is . . .
Seen Through the Lens of God's Love

And we know that all things work together for good to them that love God, to them who are called according to his purpose.

—ROMANS 8:28 KJV

Happiness is learning to live beyond the opinions of people and learning to see yourself from God's point of view. People will always have opinions. That's the way people are. But the most important thing for you is God's opinion of you. Every other opinion is secondary.

God's love for you is bigger and better than you can imagine. In fact, God's love is far too big to comprehend (in this lifetime). But this much we know: God loves you so much that He sent His Son, Jesus, to come to this earth and die for you. And, when you accepted Jesus into your heart, God gave you a gift that is more precious than gold: the gift of eternal life.

Now, precisely because you are a wondrous creation treasured by God, a question presents itself: What will you do in response to God's love? Will you ignore it or embrace it? Will you return it or neglect it? The decision, of course, is yours and yours alone.

When you embrace God's love, you are forever changed. When you embrace God's love, you feel differently about yourself, your neighbors, and your world. When you embrace God's love, you share His message and you obey His commandments.

When you accept the Father's gift of grace, you are blessed here on earth and throughout all eternity. So do yourself a favor right now: accept God's love with open arms. When you do, your life will be changed today, tomorrow, and forever.

Great Ideas About God's Love

Being loved by Him whose opinion matters most gives us the security to risk loving, too—even loving ourselves.

—GLORIA GAITHER

There is no pit so deep that God's love is not deeper still.

—CORRIE TEN BOOM

Love is not something God does; it is something God is.

—BETH MOORE

When once we are assured that God is good, then there can be nothing left to fear.

—HANNAH WHITALL SMITH

Though our feelings come and go, His love for us does not. It is not wearied by our sins, or our indifference; and, therefore, it is quite relentless in its determination that we shall be cured of those sins, at whatever cost to us, at whatever cost to Him.

—C. S. LEWIS

Life is beautiful when your eyeglasses are colored with love.

—A. R. BERNARD

More from God's Word

But the love of the Lord remains forever with those who fear him. His salvation extends to the children's children of those who are faithful to his covenant, of those who obey his commandments!

—PSALM 103:17–18 NLT

Praise him, all you people of the earth. For he loves us with unfailing love; the Lord's faithfulness endures forever. Praise the Lord!

—PSALM 117 NLT

A Simple Step

The most important opinion about your life is God's opinion. Remember that in God's eyes you're precious . . . and it's His perspective that really matters.

Your Thoughts

17

Happiness Is . . .
The Right Kind of Input

Always be happy. Never stop praying. Give thanks whatever
happens. That is what God wants for you in Christ Jesus.

— 1 THESSALONIANS 5:16–18 ICB

I f you want to be happy, if you want to be healthy, if you
want to be prosperous, if you want to have a good mar-
riage, if you want to have good relationships, if you want
to have peace of mind, how can you do it? Well, a great place
to start is by making sure that you're putting the right kind of
thoughts into your mind. If you want to enjoy better results,
you'll need to improve the quality of the input that you feed
into your brain. And the sooner you start sending the right
kind of messages in your mind, the sooner you'll begin produc-
ing the results you want.

Human nature being what it is, you'll be tempted to
think—and to behave—in undisciplined ways. But you must

resist that temptation. Otherwise, when crisis comes, you'll be tempted to imagine the worst, to plan for the worst, to expect the worst, and to live down to your expectations.

So, do yourself and your loved ones a big-league favor: Fill your mind with the right kind of input. When you do, your output will, more often than not, take care of itself.

Great Ideas About . . .
Happiness

Each one of us is responsible for our own happiness. If we choose to allow ourselves to become miserable and unhappy, the problem is ours, not someone else's.

—JOYCE MEYER

Happiness is what you think, what you say, and what you do when you are in harmony.

—GANDHI

Act as if you were already happy, and that will tend to make you happy.

—DALE CARNEGIE

Pleasure seeking is a barren business; happiness is never found till we have the grace to stop looking for it and to give our attention to persons and matters external to ourselves.

—J. I. PACKER

If you ever find happiness by hunting for it, you will find it, as the old woman did her lost spectacles, safe on her nose all the time.

—JOSH BILLINGS

Positive expectations set the atmosphere for miracles.

—A. R. BERNARD

More from God's Word

I will praise you, Lord, with all my heart. I will tell all the miracles you have done. I will be happy because of you; God Most High, I will sing praises to your name.

—PSALM 9:1-2 NCV

What joy for those who can live in your house, always singing your praises. What joy for those whose strength comes from the Lord . . .

—PSALM 84:4-5 NLT

A Simple Step

The best day to be happy is this one. Don't spend your whole life in the waiting room.

Your Thoughts

18

Happiness Is . . .
Having Hope for the Future, Having Faith in God

For I know the thoughts that I think toward you, says the Lord, thoughts of peace and not of evil, to give you a future and a hope. Then you will call upon Me and go and pray to Me, and I will listen to you.

—JEREMIAH 29:11–12 NKJV

The self-fulfilling prophecy is alive, well, and living at your house. If you trust God and have faith in the future, your optimistic beliefs will give you direction and motivation. That's one reason that you should never lose hope, but certainly not the only reason. The primary reason that you, as a believer, should never lose hope, is because of God's unfailing promises.

Make no mistake about it: Thoughts are powerful things— your thoughts have the power to lift you up or to hold you down. When you acquire the habit of hopeful thinking, you will have acquired a powerful tool for improving your life. So if you find yourself falling into the spiritual traps of worry and discouragement, be sure to redirect your thoughts. And if you fall into the terrible habit of negative thinking, think again. After all, God's Word teaches us that Christ can overcome every difficulty. And when God makes a promise, He keeps it.

Great Ideas About Hope

Three grand essentials to happiness in this life are something to do, something to love, and something to hope for.

—JOSEPH ADDISON

Hope looks for the good in people, opens doors for people, discovers what can be done to help, lights a candle, does not yield to cynicism. Hope sets people free.

—BARBARA JOHNSON

Live for today, but hold your hands open to tomorrow. Anticipate the future and its changes with joy. There is a seed of God's love in every event, every circumstance, every unpleasant situation in which you may find yourself.

—BARBARA JOHNSON

Never yield to gloomy anticipation. Place your hope and confidence in God. He has no record of failure.

—MRS. CHARLES E. COWMAN

Be hopeful! For tomorrow has never happened before.

—ROBERT SCHULLER

More from God's Word

Let us hold on to the confession of our hope without wavering, for He who promised is faithful.

—HEBREWS 10:23 HCSB

For I hope in You, O LORD; You will answer, O Lord my God.

—PSALM 38:15 NASB

A Simple Step

Jesus came to give us abundant life, to change the quality of our existence. Our job, of course, is to obey, to pray, to work, and to accept His abundance with open arms.

Your Thoughts

19

Happiness Is . . .
Learning to Worry Less and Trust God More

Have you acquired the habit of worrying about almost everything under the sun? If so, it's a habit you should break. Why? Because happiness and worry can't live together in the same human heart—they are emotions that are mutually exclusive. So if you want to be happier (not to mention healthier), you must find ways to worry less. But "worrying less" isn't always easy.

Even if you're a very faithful Christian, you may be plagued by occasional periods of discouragement and doubt. Even though you trust God's promise of salvation—even though you sincerely believe in God's love and protection—you may find yourself upset by the countless details of everyday life. Jesus understood your concerns when He spoke the reassuring words found in the sixth chapter of Matthew:

Therefore I say to you, do not worry about your life, what you will eat or what you will drink; nor about your body, what you will put on. Is not life more than food and the body more than clothing? Look at the birds of the air, for they neither sow nor reap nor gather into barns; yet your heavenly Father feeds them. Are you not of more value than they? Which of you by worrying can add one cubit to his stature? . . . Therefore do not worry about tomorrow, for tomorrow will worry about its own things. Sufficient for the day is its own trouble. (vv. 25–27, 34 NKJV)

Where is the best place to take your worries? Take them to God. Take your troubles to Him; take your fears to Him; take your doubts to Him; take your weaknesses to Him; take your sorrows to Him . . . and leave them all there. Seek protection from the One who offers you eternal salvation; build your spiritual house upon the Rock that cannot be moved.

Perhaps you are concerned about your future, your relationships, or your finances. Or perhaps you are simply a "worrier" by nature. If so, choose to make Matthew 6 a regular part of your daily Bible reading. This beautiful passage will remind you that God still sits in His heaven and you are His beloved child. Then, perhaps, you will worry a little less and trust God a little more, and that's as it should be, because God is trustworthy . . . and you are protected.

Great Ideas About
Worrying Less and Trusting God More

Remember always that there are two things which are more utterly incompatible even than oil and water, and these two are trust and worry.

—HANNAH WHITALL SMITH

There are two kinds of worries—those you can do something about and those you can't. Don't spend any time on the latter.

—DUKE ELLINGTON

Worry is simply thinking the same thing over and over again . . . and not doing anything about it.

—BRANCH RICKEY

Come up from the lowlands; there are heights yet to climb. You cannot do healthful thinking in the lowlands. Look to the mountaintop for faith.

—MARY MCLEOD BETHUNE

Pray, and let God worry.

—MARTIN LUTHER

Worry is no substitute for prayer.

—A. R. BERNARD

More from God's Word

Do not worry about anything, but pray and ask God for everything you need, always giving thanks.

—PHILIPPIANS 4:6 NCV

Give your worries to the Lord, and he will take care of you. He will never let good people down.

—PSALM 55:22 NCV

A Simple Step

Focus on your work, not your worries: Worry is never a valid substitute for work. So get out there, do your best, and leave the rest up to God.

Your Thoughts

_____
_____
_____
_____
_____
_____
_____
_____
_____
_____
_____
_____
_____
_____
_____
_____
_____
_____
_____
_____
_____
_____
_____
_____

20

Happiness Is . . .
Learning to Rejoice

Rejoice in the Lord always. Again I will say, rejoice!

—PHILIPPIANS 4:4 NKJV

Have you made the choice to rejoice? If you're a Christian, you have every reason to be joyful. After all, the ultimate battle has already been won on the cross at Calvary. And if your life has been transformed by Christ's sacrifice, then you, as a recipient of God's grace, have every reason to live joyfully. Yet sometimes, amid the inevitable hustle and bustle of life here on earth, you may lose sight of your blessings as you wrestle with the challenges of everyday life.

Do you seek happiness, abundance, and contentment? If so, here are some things you should do: Love God and His Son; depend upon God for strength; try, to the best of your abilities,

to follow God's will; and strive to obey His Holy Word. When you do these things, you'll discover that happiness goes hand-in-hand with righteousness. The happiest people are not those who rebel against God; the happiest people are those who love God and obey His commandments.

What does life have in store for you? A world full of possibilities (of course, it's up to you to seize them) and God's promise of abundance (of course, it's up to you to accept it). So, as you embark upon the next phase of your journey, remember to celebrate the life that God has given you.

Great Ideas About Joy

If you can forgive the person you were, accept the person you are, and believe in the person you will become, you are headed for joy. So celebrate your life.

—BARBARA JOHNSON

The Christian lifestyle is not one of legalistic do's and don'ts, but one that is positive, attractive, and joyful.

—VONETTE BRIGHT

Joy is the direct result of having God's perspective on our daily lives and the effect of loving our Lord enough to obey His commands and trust His promises.

—BILL BRIGHT

Our sense of joy, satisfaction, and fulfillment in life increases, no matter what the circumstances, if we are in the center of God's will.

—BILLY GRAHAM

Talk happiness. The world is sad enough without your woes.

—ELLA WHEELER WILCOX

More from God's Word

Rejoice, and be exceeding glad: for great is your reward in heaven.

—MATTHEW 5:12 KJV

I will praise you, Lord, with all my heart; I will tell of all the marvelous things you have done. I will be filled with joy because of you. I will sing praises to your name, O Most High.

—PSALM 9:1–2 NLT

For this day is holy unto our Lord; neither be ye sorry, for the joy of the Lord is your strength.

—NEHEMIAH 8:10B KJV

A Simple Step

Joy does not depend upon your circumstances; it depends upon your thoughts and upon your relationship with God.

Your Thoughts

_____
_____
_____
_____
_____
_____
_____
_____
_____
_____
_____
_____
_____
_____
_____
_____
_____
_____
_____
_____
_____
_____
_____
_____
_____
_____

21

Happiness Is . . . Learning Not to Judge Others

Do not judge, and you will not be judged. Do not condemn, and
you will not be condemned. Forgive, and you will be forgiven.

—LUKE 6:37 HCSB

Would you like a surefire formula for being unhappy? Here it is: Spend as much time as you can judging other people. But if you'd rather be happy, please remember this: In matters of judgment, God does not need (or want) your help. Why? Because God is perfectly capable of judging the human heart . . . while you are not. This message was made clear by the teachings of Jesus.

As Jesus came upon a young woman who had been condemned by the Pharisees, He spoke not only to the crowd that was gathered there, but also to all generations, when He warned, "He that is without sin among you, let him first cast a stone at her" (John 8:7 KJV).

Christ's message is straightforward: Because we are all sin-

ners, we are commanded to refrain from judging others. Yet the irony is this: It is precisely because we are sinners that we are so quick to judge.

All of us have fallen short of God's laws, and none of us, therefore, is qualified to "cast the first stone." Thankfully, God has forgiven us, and we, too, must forgive others. Let us refrain, then, from judging our family members, our friends, and our loved ones. Instead, let us forgive them and love them in the same way that God has forgiven us.

Great Ideas About Judging Others

God is the only judge. You are just his emissary of peace.

—ST. THÉRÈSE OF LISIEUX

Being critical of others, including God, is one way we try to avoid facing and judging our own sins.

—WARREN WIERSBE

Turn your attention upon yourself and beware of judging the deeds of other men, for in judging others a man labors vainly, often makes mistakes, and easily sins; whereas, in judging and taking stock of himself he does something that is always profitable.

—THOMAS À KEMPIS

Too many Christians think they are prosecuting attorneys or judges, when, in reality, God has called all of us to be witnesses.

—WARREN WIERSBE

Don't judge other people more harshly than you want God to judge you.

—MARIE T. FREEMAN

When we are of a critical spirit we tend to judge others by their actions and ourselves by our intentions. So we condemn others and excuse ourselves.

—A. R. BERNARD

More from God's Word

Why do you look at the speck of sawdust in your brother's eye and pay no attention to the plank in your own eye? How can you say to your brother, "Let me take the speck out of your eye," when all the time there is a plank in your own eye? You hypocrite, first take the plank out of your own eye, and then you will see clearly to remove the speck from your brother's eye.

—MATTHEW 7:3–5 NIV

You, therefore, have no excuse, you who pass judgment on someone else, for at whatever point you judge the other, you are condemning yourself.

—ROMANS 2:1 NIV

A Simple Step

Your ability to judge others requires a divine insight that you simply don't have. So do everybody (including yourself) a favor: Don't judge.

Your Thoughts

22

Happiness Is . . .
Love

*And now abide faith, hope, love, these three; but the greatest of
these is love.*

— I CORINTHIANS 13:13 NKJV

Happiness means gaining an awareness of the tremen-
dously positive power of love. And if there's anything
that Jesus brought to this world, it was an awareness
of the transformational power of love.

Love is a choice. Either you choose to behave lovingly
toward others . . . or not; either you behave yourself in ways
that enhance your relationships . . . or not. But make no mistake: Genuine love requires effort. If you want to build relationships that last, you must be willing to do your part.

Since the days of Adam and Eve, God has allowed His
children to make choices for themselves, and so it is with you.
As you interact with family and friends, you have choices to

make . . . lots of them. If you choose wisely, you'll be happier and healthier; if you choose unwisely, you'll bear the consequences.

God does not intend for you to experience mediocre relationships; He created you for far greater things. Building lasting relationships requires compassion, wisdom, empathy, kindness, courtesy, and forgiveness. If that sounds a lot like work, it is—which is perfectly fine with God. Why? Because He knows that you are capable of doing that work, and because He knows that the fruits of those labors will bring a rich harvest to you and to your loved ones.

Great Ideas About Love

Love wins when everything else will fail.

—FANNY JACKSON COPPIN

He who is filled with love is filled with God Himself.

—ST. AUGUSTINE

Love stretches your heart and makes you big inside.

—MARGARET WALKER

Carve your name on hearts, not on marble.

—C. H. SPURGEON

There is always something left to love. And if you ain't learned that, you ain't learned nothing.

—LORRAINE HANSBERRY

Love is the desire to benefit others at the expense of self.

—EDWIN LOUIS COLE

Love is a commitment based on a decision. Love is not centered in the emotions; it is centered in the will. We love because we choose to, or choose not to.

—A. R. BERNARD

More from God's Word

Love one another deeply, from the heart.

—1 PETER 1:22 NIV

Above all, love each other deeply, because love covers over a multitude of sins.

—1 PETER 4:8 NIV

A Simple Step

The key to successful Christian living lies in your submission to the Spirit of God. If you call yourself a Christian, then God has commanded you to love people . . . and it's a commandment that covers both saints and sinners.

23

Happiness Is . . .
Living in the Now

This is the day the Lord has made; let us rejoice and be glad in it.
—PSALM 118:24 HCSB

ll too often, people think of happiness as something that has already happened (in the distant past) or something that may occur "someday" (in the distant future)—but they're mistaken. Happiness, if it occurs at all, occurs in the present tense; happiness takes place in the precious present.

Are you willing to celebrate your life today? You should. After all, this day is a blessed gift from God. And when you stop to think about it, you probably have countless reasons to rejoice. Yet on some days, when the demands of life threaten to overwhelm you, you may not feel much like rejoicing. Instead of celebrating God's gifts, you may find yourself frustrated by the obligations of today and worried by the uncertainties of tomorrow. If so, it's time to redirect your

thoughts to things positive . . . and it's time to start counting your blessings.

The familiar words of Psalm 118:24 remind us that this is the day the Lord has made, and we should rejoice. So whatever this day holds for you, begin it and end it with God as your partner. And throughout the day, give thanks to the One who created you. God's love for you is infinite. Accept it joyfully . . . and be happy. Now.

Great Ideas About the Present

The present is holy ground.

—ALFRED NORTH WHITEHEAD

Whatever I'm doing, I don't think in terms of tomorrow. I try to live in the present moment.

—ANITA BAKER

Exhaust the little moment. Soon it dies.

—GWENDOLYN BROOKS

I depend on the integrity and the faithfulness of God to make each moment as meaningful as He can and as I allow.

—BILL BRIGHT

People create success in their lives by focusing on today. It may

sound trite, but today is the only time you have. It's too late for yesterday. And you can't depend on tomorrow.

—JOHN MAXWELL

All you have is today because when tomorrow comes, it will still be today.

—A. R. BERNARD

More from God's Word

Since everything here today might well be gone tomorrow, do you see how essential it is to live a holy life?

—2 PETER 3:11 MSG

While it is daytime, we must continue doing the work of the One who sent me. Night is coming, when no one can work.

—JOHN 9:4 NCV

A Simple Step

If you had to be the person you are today for the rest of your life, would you be happy? If the answer is "Absolutely!" keep up the good work. But if the answer is "Maybe"—or, for that matter, an outright "No"—then it's time to take responsibility for your future . . . and it's time to start making changes now.

Your Thoughts

24

Happiness Is . . .
Activity with Purpose

May He give you what your heart desires and fulfill your whole
purpose.

—PSALM 20:4 HCSB

appiness is activity with purpose. And purpose, like everything else in the universe, begins in the heart of God. Whether you realize it or not, God has a direction for your life, a divine calling, a path along which He intends to lead you. When you welcome God into your heart and establish a genuine relationship with Him, He will begin—and He will continue—to make His purposes known.

Have you ever felt that you were just spinning your wheels? Just going through the motions? If so, you know that there's no fulfillment in purposeless living. Your job, therefore, is to keep searching for God's purpose in your life . . . and to keep searching until you find it.

Discovering God's unfolding purpose for your life is a daily journey, a journey guided by the teachings of God's Holy Word. As you reflect upon God's promises and upon the meaning that those promises hold for you, ask God to lead you throughout the coming day. Let your Heavenly Father direct your steps; concentrate on what God wants you to do now, and leave the distant future in hands that are far more capable than your own: His hands.

Sometimes, God's intentions will be clear to you; other times, God's plan will seem uncertain at best. But even on those difficult days when you are unsure which way to turn, you must never lose sight of these overriding facts: God created you for a reason; He has important work for you to do; and He's waiting patiently for you to do it. So why not begin today?

Great Ideas About Purpose

Many persons have a wrong idea of what constitutes true happiness. It is not attained through self-gratification, but through fidelity to a worthy purpose.

—HELEN KELLER

Continually restate to yourself what the purpose of your life is.

—OSWALD CHAMBERS

What we need are mental and spiritual giants who are aflame with a purpose.

—NANNIE BURROUGHS

Without God, life has no purpose, and without purpose, life has no meaning.

—RICK WARREN

Happiness is not a goal; it is a by-product.

—ELEANOR ROOSEVELT

Life is better when organized around purpose.

—A. R. BERNARD

More from God's Word

For it is God who is working in you, both to will and to act for His good purpose.

—PHILIPPIANS 2:13 HCSB

We look at this Son and see the God who cannot be seen. We look at this Son and see God's original purpose in everything created.

—COLOSSIANS 1:15 MSG

A Simple Step

Ten years from now you will be somewhere—the question is, Where? You have the power to make that determination. And remember: It's not about earning a living; it's about designing a life.

Your Thoughts

25

Happiness Is . . .
Using Your Talents

The man who had received the five talents brought the other five.
"Master," he said, "you entrusted me with five talents. See, I
have gained five more." His master replied, "Well done, good and
faithful servant! You have been faithful with a few things; I will
put you in charge of many things. Come and share your master's
happiness."

—MATTHEW 25:20-21 NIV

I f you squander your talents, you'll never really be happy. So
here's a question for you: Are you really using the talents
that God has given you, or are you just coasting through
life?

God knew precisely what He was doing when He gave
you a unique set of talents and opportunities. And now, your
Heavenly Father wants you to be a faithful steward of the gifts
He has given you. But you live in a society that may encourage

you to do otherwise. You face countless temptations to squander your time, your resources, and your talents. So you must be keenly aware of the inevitable distractions that can waste your energy, your time, your talents, and your opportunities.

Every day of your life, you have a choice to make: to nurture your talents or neglect them. When you choose wisely, God rewards your efforts, and He expands your opportunities to serve Him.

God has blessed you with unique opportunities to serve Him, and He has given you every tool that you need to do so. Today, accept this challenge: Value the talent that God has given you, nourish it, make it grow, and share it with the world. After all, the best way to say "Thank you" for God's gifts is to use them.

Great Ideas About Talents

Just don't give up trying to do what you really want to do. Where there's love and inspiration, I don't think you can go wrong.

—ELLA FITZGERALD

In the long run, it makes little difference how cleverly others are deceived; if we are not doing what we are best equipped to do, there will be a core of unhappiness in our lives which will be more and more difficult to ignore as the years pass.

—DOROTHEA BRANDE

Happiness lies in the joy of achievement and the thrill of creative effort.

—FRANKLIN D. ROOSEVELT

Everyone has a talent for something.

—MARIAN ANDERSON

The secret of a happy life is to do your duty and trust in God.

—SAM JONES

Waste your talents and you waste your life.

—A. R. BERNARD

More from God's Word

Do not neglect the gift that is in you.

—1 TIMOTHY 4:14 HCSB

I remind you to keep ablaze the gift of God that is in you.

—2 TIMOTHY 1:6 HCSB

A Simple Step

You are the sole owner of your own set of talents and opportunities. God has given you your own particular gifts—the rest is up to you.

Your Thoughts

26

Happiness Is . . .
A Thankful Heart

*Enter into His gates with thanksgiving, and into His courts with
praise. Be thankful to Him, and bless His name. For the Lord is
good; His mercy is everlasting, and His truth endures to all generations.*

—PSALM 100:4-5 NKJV

Thankful people are happy people. Are you a thankful
person? Do you appreciate the gifts that God has given
you? And do you demonstrate your gratitude by being a
faithful steward of the gifts and talents that you have received
from your Creator? You most certainly should be thankful.
After all, when you stop to think about it, God has given you
more blessings than you can count. So the question of the day
is this: Will you thank your Heavenly Father . . . or will you
spend your time and energy doing other things?

The coming day is a canvas upon which you can compose

a beautiful work of art if you choose to do so. So today, look for good things to do and good things to be thankful for. If you look carefully, you won't need to look very far. And remember: When it comes time to count your blessings, nobody can count them for you.

God is always listening—are you willing to say thanks? It's up to you, and the next move is always yours.

Great Ideas About Thanksgiving

Any day I wake up is a good day.

—DUKE ELLINGTON

No duty is more urgent than that of returning thanks.

—ST. AMBROSE

Thanksgiving or complaining—these words express two contrastive attitudes of the souls of God's children in regard to His dealings with them. . . . The soul that gives thanks can find comfort in everything; the soul that complains can find comfort in nothing.

—HANNAH WHITALL SMITH

When it comes to life, the critical thing is whether you take things for granted or take them with gratitude.

—G. K. CHESTERTON

God gave you a gift of 86,400 seconds today. Have you used
one to say thank you?

—WILLIAM ARTHUR WARD

Gratitude confirms relationships.

—EDWIN LOUIS COLE

More from God's Word

Thanks be to God for His indescribable gift.

—2 CORINTHIANS 9:15 HCSB

It is good to give thanks to the Lord, And to sing praises to Your
name, O Most High.

—PSALM 92:1 NKJV

A Simple Step

*God gives each of us more blessings than we can count. Those
blessings include life, family, freedom, friends, talents, and
possessions, just for starters. Winners recognize the size and
scope of God's blessings—and real winners (like you) spend plenty
of time thanking Him.*

Your Thoughts

27

Happiness Is . . .
A Way of Mind

Finally brothers, whatever is true, whatever is honorable, what-
ever is just, whatever is pure, whatever is lovely, whatever is
commendable—if there is any moral excellence and if there is
any praise—dwell on these things.

—PHILIPPIANS 4:8 HCSB

imply put, happiness is a way of thinking. So here's the big question: How will you direct your thoughts today? Will you obey the words of Philippians 4:8 by dwelling upon those things that are honorable, true, and worthy of praise? Or will you allow your thoughts to be hijacked by the negativity that seems to dominate our troubled world?

Are you fearful, angry, bored, or worried? Are you so pre-occupied with the concerns of this day that you fail to thank God for the promise of eternity? Are you confused, bitter, or pessimistic? If so, God wants to have a little talk with you.

God intends that you be an ambassador for Him, an enthusiastic, hope-filled Christian. But God won't force you to adopt a positive attitude. It's up to you to think positively about your blessings and opportunities . . . or not. So, today and every day hereafter, celebrate this life that God has given you by focusing your thoughts and your energies upon "things that are excellent and worthy of praise." Today, count your blessings instead of your hardships. And thank the Giver of all things good for gifts that are simply too numerous to count.

Great Ideas About Thoughts

Happiness doesn't depend upon who you are or what you have; it depends on what you think.

—DALE CARNEGIE

The greater part of our happiness or misery depends on our dispositions and not our circumstances.

—MARTHA WASHINGTON

Every good thought you think is contributing its share to the ultimate result of your life.

—GRENVILLE KLEISER

I am happy and content because I think I am.

—ALAIN

Our life is what our thoughts make it.

—MARCUS AURELIUS

Positive thoughts are the seeds for great achievements.

—A. R. BERNARD

More from God's Word

So prepare your minds for service and have self-control.

—1 PETER 1:13 NCV

Those who are pure in their thinking are happy, because they will be with God.

—MATTHEW 5:8 NCV

A Simple Step

Happiness is a positive interpretation of the world and its events. Happiness requires that you train yourself to see the good in everything, no matter what happens.

Your Thoughts

28

Happiness Is . . .
Finding Wisdom and Understanding

Joyful is the person who finds wisdom, the one who gains under-
standing.

—PROVERBS 3:13 NLT

Happiness begins with wisdom and understanding. In other words, happiness and wisdom are traveling companions. But here's a word of warning: The acquisition of wisdom is seldom easy or quick.

Wisdom is not like a mushroom; it does not spring up overnight. It is, instead, like an oak tree that starts as a tiny acorn, grows into a sapling, and eventually reaches up to the sky, tall and strong.

Do you seek wisdom? Then seek it every day of your life. Seek it with consistency and purpose. And seek it in the right place. That place, of course, is, first and foremost, the Word of God.

Sometimes, amid the demands of daily life, you will lose perspective. Life may seem out of balance, and the pressures of everyday living may seem overwhelming. What's needed is a fresh perspective, a restored sense of balance . . . and God's wisdom. If you call upon the Lord and seek to see the world through His eyes, He will give you guidance and perspective. If you make God's priorities your priorities, He will lead you along a path of His choosing. If you study God's teachings, you will be reminded that God's reality is the ultimate reality.

As you accumulate wisdom, you may feel the need to share your insights with friends and family members. If so, remember this: Your actions must reflect the values that you hold dear. The best way to share your wisdom—perhaps the only way—is not by your words, but by your example.

So if you're really interested in being a happier person, then you must make up your mind to become a wiser person. It's the only way.

Great Ideas About Wisdom

The wisest mind has something yet to learn.

—GEORGE SANTAYANA

Follow your instincts. That is where true wisdom manifests itself.

—OPRAH WINFREY

Don't expect wisdom to come into your life like great chunks of rock on a conveyor belt. Wisdom comes privately from God as a by-product of right decisions, godly reactions, and the application of spiritual principles to daily circumstances.

—CHARLES SWINDOLL

Knowledge is horizontal. Wisdom is vertical; it comes down from above.

—BILLY GRAHAM

No one is truly happy if he has what he wants, but only if he wants something he should have.

—ST. AUGUSTINE

More from God's Word

"Therefore everyone who hears these words of mine and puts them into practice is like a wise man who built his house on the rock."

—JESUS, MATTHEW 7:24 NIV

But the wisdom that is from above is first pure, then peaceable, gentle, willing to yield, full of mercy and good fruits, without partiality and without hypocrisy.

—JAMES 3:17 NKJV

If you need wisdom, ask our generous God, and He will give it to you. He will not rebuke you for asking.

—JAMES 1:5 NLT

A Simple Step

Wisdom isn't just knowing what to do—it's doing what you know.
Jesus said, "If ye know these things, happy are ye if ye do them"
(John 13:17 KJV).

Your Thoughts

_____

_____

_____

_____

_____

_____

_____

_____

_____

_____

_____

_____

_____

_____

_____

_____

_____

_____

29

Happiness Is . . . Doing What Needs to Be Done

But be doers of the word, and not hearers only, deceiving
yourselves.

—JAMES 1:22 NKJV

If you'd like another simple prescription for finding—and keeping—happiness, here it is: Learn to do first things first and learn to do them sooner rather than later. Otherwise, you'll be like a dog constantly chasing his tail, spinning in circles, going nowhere.

Are you in the habit of doing what needs to be done when it needs to be done, or are you a dues-paying member of the Procrastinators' Club? If you've acquired the habit of doing your most important work first (even if you'd rather be doing something else), congratulations! But, if you find yourself putting off all those unpleasant tasks until later (or never), it's time to think about the consequences of your behavior.

Chronic procrastinators unintentionally squeeze the joy out of their own lives and the lives of their loved ones. So your job is to summon the determination, the courage, and the wisdom to defeat Old Man Procrastination whenever he arrives at your doorstep.

You can free yourself from the emotional quicksand by paying less attention to your fears and more attention to your responsibilities. So, when you're faced with a difficult choice or an unpleasant responsibility, don't spend endless hours fretting over your fate. Simply seek God's counsel and get busy. When you do, you will be richly rewarded because of your willingness to act.

Great Ideas About Action

We cannot do everything at once, but we can do something at once.

—CALVIN COOLIDGE

Life is far more flexible than it seems to those who are unwilling to act.

—DOROTHEA BRANDE

You cannot run away from weakness; you must sometimes fight it out or perish. And if that be so, why not now, and where you stand?

—ROBERT LOUIS STEVENSON

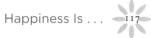

Do the thing we fear and the death of fear is certain.

—RALPH WALDO EMERSON

When people made up their minds that they wanted to be free and took action, there was a change.

—ROSA PARKS

Git 'er done!

—TEXAS SAYING

More from God's Word

Therefore, get your minds ready for action, being self-disciplined, and set your hope completely on the grace to be brought to you at the revelation of Jesus Christ.

—1 PETER 1:13 HCSB

Are there those among you who are truly wise and understanding? Then they should show it by living right and doing good things with a gentleness that comes from wisdom.

—JAMES 3:13 NCV

A Simple Step

Today pick out one important obligation that you've been putting off. Then take at least one specific step toward the completion of the task you've been avoiding. Even if you don't finish the job, you'll discover that it's easier to get started than you think.

Your Thoughts

30

Happiness Is . . .
Avoiding the Traps of the World

Do not love the world or the things that belong to the world. If anyone loves the world, love for the Father is not in him.

— I JOHN 2:15 HCSB

All of mankind is engaged in a colossal, worldwide treasure hunt. Some folks seek treasure from earthly sources, treasures such as material wealth or public acclaim—these folks don't find enduring happiness, because they're searching for it in the wrong places. Other people seek happiness by making God's promises the cornerstone of their lives—and these folks are blessed by the Creator.

What kind of treasure hunter are you? Are you so caught up in the demands of popular society that you sometimes allow the search for worldly treasures to become your primary focus? If so, it's time to reorganize your daily to-do list by placing God in His rightful place: first place.

If you sincerely seek to strengthen your character, you'll focus more intently on God's treasures and less intently on the world's treasures. Don't allow anyone or anything to separate you from your Heavenly Father and His only begotten Son.

Society's priorities are transitory; God's priorities are permanent. The world's treasures are difficult to find and difficult to keep; God's treasures are ever-present and everlasting. Which treasures and whose priorities will you claim as your own? The answer should be obvious.

Great Ideas About Worldliness

I'm fulfilled in what I do. . . . I never thought that a lot of money or fine clothes—the finer things of life—would make you happy. My concept of happiness is to be filled in a spiritual sense.

—CORETTA SCOTT KING

Too many Christians have geared their program to please, to entertain, and to gain favor from this world. We are concerned with how much, instead of how little, like this age we can become.

—BILLY GRAHAM

Aim at heaven and you will get earth thrown in. Aim at earth and you get neither.

—C. S. LEWIS

The doors of wisdom are never shut.

—BEN FRANKLIN

Don't mistake pleasure for happiness.

—JOSH BILLINGS

Your greatest value in life is your value to God, and it's not measured in dollars and cents.

—A. R. BERNARD

More from God's Word

For whatever is born of God overcomes the world. And this is the victory that has overcome the world—our faith.

—1 JOHN 5:4 NKJV

Religion that God our Father accepts as pure and faultless is this: to look after orphans and widows in their distress and to keep oneself from being polluted by the world.

—JAMES 1:27 NIV

A Simple Step

If you dwell on the world's messages, you're setting yourself up for disaster. If you dwell on God's message, you're setting yourself up for victory.

A. R. Bernard

Your Thoughts

31

Happiness Is . . .
Finding the Courage to Dream

With God's power working in us, God can do much, much more than anything we can ask or imagine.

—EPHESIANS 3:20 NCV

Your Heavenly Father created you with unique gifts and untapped talents; your job is to tap them. When you do, you'll begin to feel an increasing sense of confidence in yourself and in your future. And you'll be happier, too.

On occasion, you will face the inevitable disappointments of life. And sometimes, you must endure life-altering personal losses that leave you breathless. On such occasions, you may be tempted to abandon your dreams. Don't do it! Instead, trust that God is preparing you for greater things.

Concentration camp survivor Corrie Ten Boom observed,

"Every experience God gives us, every person he brings into our lives, is the perfect preparation for the future that only he can see." These words apply to you.

It takes courage to dream big dreams. You will discover that courage when you do three things: accept the past, trust God to manage the future, and make the most of the time He has given you today.

Nothing is too difficult for God, and no dreams are too big for Him—not even yours. So start living—and dreaming—accordingly.

Great Ideas About Dreams

The future belongs to those who believe in the beauty of their dreams.

—ELEANOR ROOSEVELT

Too many people put their dreams "on hold." It takes an uncommon amount of guts to put your dreams on the line, to hold them up and say, "How good or bad am I?" That's where the courage comes in.

—ERMA BOMBECK

Since it doesn't cost a dime to dream, you'll never shortchange yourself when you stretch your imagination.

—ROBERT SCHULLER

You don't always reach a dream in the way you first see it. When you get there, it's a different dream, but it's still a dream.

—TINA TURNER

If you can dream it, you can do it.

—WALT DISNEY

Without a vision for the future, you will always live in the past.

—A. R. BERNARD

More from God's Word

Where there is no vision, the people perish. . . .

—PROVERBS 29:18 KJV

Hope deferred makes the heart sick, but a dream fulfilled is a tree of life.

—PROVERBS 13:12 NLT

"In the last days," God says, "I will pour out my Spirit on all people. Your sons and daughters will prophesy. Your young men will see visions, and your old men will dream dreams."

—ACTS 2:17 NLT

A Simple Step

Making your dreams come true requires work. John Maxwell writes, "The gap between your vision and your present reality can only be filled through a commitment to maximize your potential." Enough said.

Your Thoughts

32

Happiness Is . . .
Aging Wisely and Gracefully

Youth may be admired for vigor, but gray hair gives prestige to
old age.

—PROVERBS 20:29 MSG

We live in a society that glorifies youth. The messages that we receive from the media are unrelenting: We are told that we must do everything within our power to retain youthful values and a youthful appearance. The goal, we are told, is to remain "forever young"—yet this goal is not only unrealistic, it is also unworthy of women who understand what genuine beauty is, and what it isn't.

As you consider what aging means to you, please consider the following: It's inevitable. Since aging is a fact of life, you should strive to come to terms with it sooner rather than later.

The media focuses on appearances . . . but you should focus on substance, beginning with your spiritual health, your

mental health, your physical fitness, and the health of your relationships.

Messages from the media . . . the media is in the business of selling things, so the media wants to convince you that you're not "good enough" until you buy its "new and improved" products. Oftentimes, these products are accompanied by advertisements that make bold promises—promises to stop Father Time in his tracks. These messages are not based upon truth; they're based upon someone's desire to sell you products that you probably don't need . . . so beware.

When it comes to "health and beauty," you should focus more on health than on beauty. In fact, when you take care of your physical, spiritual, and mental health, your appearance will tend to take care of itself.

Talk it over with God: The next time you bow your head in prayer, ask your Heavenly Father if His love is contingent upon your age or appearance. And then, when you've been assured that God loves you during every stage of life, embrace the aging process for what it is: an opportunity to grow closer to your loved ones and to your Creator.

Great Ideas About Aging

To know how to grow old is the masterwork of wisdom, and one of the most difficult chapters in the great art of living.

—HENRI FRÉDÉRIC AMIEL

The real trick is to stay alive as long as you live.

—ANN LANDERS

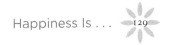

Longevity is both physical and mental.

—PLACIDO DOMINGO

Surely the consolation prize of old age is finding out how few things are worth worrying over.

—DOROTHY DIX

If you asked me the secret to longevity, I would tell you that you have to work at taking care of your health. But a lot of it's attitude, too. I am alive out of sheer determination, honey!

—BESSIE DELANY

Growing older is inevitable; growing wiser is a choice.

—A. R. BERNARD

More from God's Word

Teach us to number our days carefully so that we may develop wisdom in our hearts.

—PSALM 90:12 HCSB

Therefore we do not give up; even though our outer person is being destroyed, our inner person is being renewed day by day.

—2 CORINTHIANS 4:16 HCSB

A Simple Step

Your body continues to grow older every day. But you can keep your heart and mind young—it's up to you to do the work that's required to stay physically fit and fully engaged with life.

Your Thoughts

33

Happiness Is . . .
Freedom from Procrastination

If you wait for perfect conditions, you will never get anything done.

—ECCLESIASTES 11:4 TLB

Procrastination is so common among college students that one university actually set up counseling services to help students overcome it. In an article on the school's website, psychologist William Knaust estimated that 90 percent of college students procrastinate—of these young procrastinators, 25 percent are chronic offenders who often end up dropping out of college.

What does procrastination mean to you? I define it as "The avoidance of a task that needs to be accomplished—this avoidance behavior usually leads to feelings of guilt, inadequacy, depression, and self-doubt."

Why do people procrastinate? Sometimes it's simple: Procrastinators have often acquired very poor time manage-

ment habits. Chronic procrastinators usually have difficulty setting priorities, goals, and objectives. As a result they may become
overwhelmed by relatively small tasks, so instead of tackling the
job at hand, they give up before they get started.

Another reason that folks put things off is because of the
fear and anxiety that comes from their own negative self-beliefs.
They tell themselves, "I don't measure up to the task." Or "I
feel totally inadequate." Or "I'll never be good enough to do the
job right." The list of negative self-proclamations is almost endless. So instead of risking failure, these self-styled critics just keep
putting things off, with predictably unhappy results.

If you've acquired the habit of procrastination, you know
what a destructive habit it can be. And when you stop to think
about it, you have to admit that procrastination interferes with
your own happiness. After all, many of the things you keep putting off have the potential to improve your life.

Maybe you've avoided going back to finish school. Or
perhaps you "just haven't gotten around to" searching for a
better job. Or maybe you've been hindered by a hundred
other emotional roadblocks too numerous to mention. If so,
it's appropriate to ask yourself what you've been waiting for,
and why.

If you're waiting for the conditions to be perfect (or, for that
matter, if you're waiting for yourself to become perfect), it's time
for a large, sobering dose of reality. When it comes to improving
yourself or your situation, the timing is never "perfect." But it's

always the right time to take positive steps to improve your own life or the lives of your loved ones.

Overcoming procrastination begins when you honestly examine your feelings toward the task at hand. So ask yourself, "Are my feelings valid? Or am I exaggerating my own fears of inadequacy while at the same time imagining that everything must be perfect before I can begin?" And while you're at it, ask yourself if you're afraid to fail.

Happiness is understanding that failure is the womb for success. Happiness is understanding that conditions are never "perfect" for doing anything in this life. (I remember one young man who told me he was waiting to save enough money to get married. I told him, "You'll never get married!")

Happiness is freedom from fear and from all of the negative children of fear—all those nonsensical, inappropriate, overblown fears that have heretofore caused you to put things off. Procrastination is the thief of time and the grave of opportunity.

Face facts: There will always be obstacles in the way of your success. But please don't focus too intently on those obstacles; focus, instead, on your goal. Decide what you want to do; get serious, get smart; and then do it. Now!

Great Ideas About Procrastination

Procrastination is the Devil's chloroform.

—ANONYMOUS

"One of these days" is none of these days.

—ATTRIBUTED TO HENRI TUBACH AND H. G. BOHN

Never put off till tomorrow what can be done today.

—THOMAS JEFFERSON

Procrastination is the thief of time.

—EDWARD YOUNG

Putting off an easy thing makes it hard, and putting off a hard one makes it impossible.

—GEORGE H. LORIMER

Don't duck the most difficult problems. That just insures that the hardest part will be left when you're most tired. Get the big one done, and it's all downhill from then on.

—NORMAN VINCENT PEALE

Do noble things, not dream them all day long.

—CHARLES KINGSLEY

More from God's Word

Take a lesson from the ants, you lazybones. Learn from their ways and become wise! Though they have no prince or governor or ruler to make them work, they labor hard all summer, gathering food for the winter. But you, lazybones, how long will you sleep? When will you wake up? A little extra sleep, a little more slumber, a little folding of the hands to rest—then poverty

will pounce on you like a bandit; scarcity will attack you like an
armed robber.

—PROVERBS 6:11 NLT

A Simple Step
Tips for Getting Things Done

1. *Have a clear understanding of your short- and long-term
   goals, and set your priorities in accordance with those goals.*

2. *When faced with distasteful tasks, do them immediately,
   preferably first thing in the morning (even if the
   unpleasantness is a low-priority activity, go ahead and get it
   out of the way if it can be completed quickly). Dispatching
   distasteful tasks sooner rather than later will improve the
   quality of your day and prevent you from wasting untold
   amounts of energy in the process of fighting against yourself.*

3. *Avoid the trap of perfectionism. Be willing to do your best,
   and be satisfied with the results.*

4. *If you don't already own one, purchase a daily or weekly
   planning system that fits your needs. If used properly, a
   planning calendar is worth many times what you pay for it.*

5. *Start each work day with a written "to-do" list, ranked
   according to importance. At lunch time, take a moment to
   collect your thoughts, reexamine your list, and refocus your
   efforts on the most important things you wish to accomplish
   during the remainder of the day.*

Your Thoughts

34

Happiness Is . . .
Coming to Grips with Who You Really Are

Blessed is the man who does not condemn himself.

—ROMANS 14:22 HCSB

Happiness means coming to grips with who you really are and why you're really here. When God made you, He equipped you with an array of talents and abilities that are uniquely yours. It's up to you to discover those talents and to use them, but sometimes the world will encourage you to do otherwise. At times, our society will attempt to cubbyhole you, to standardize you, and to make you fit into a particular, preformed mold. Perhaps God has other plans.

Have you found something in this life that you're passionate about? Something that inspires you to jump out of bed in the morning and hit the ground running? And does your

work honor the Creator by making His world a better place? If so, congratulations: You're using your gifts well.

Sometimes, because you're a fallible human being, you may become so wrapped up in meeting society's expectations that you fail to focus on God's expectations. To do so is a mistake of major proportions—don't make it. Instead, seek God's guidance as you focus your energies on becoming the best "you" that you can possibly be.

What's the best way to thank God for the gifts that He has given you? By using them. And you might as well start using them today.

Great Ideas About Self-acceptance

One of the greatest moments in anybody's developing experience is when he no longer tries to hide from himself but determines to get acquainted with himself as he really is.

—NORMAN VINCENT PEALE

Self-trust is the first secret of success.

—RALPH WALDO EMERSON

Life is a journey; every experience is here to teach you more fully how to be who you really are.

—OPRAH WINFREY

Once you understand what your work is and you do not try to avert your eyes from it, but attempt to invest energy in getting that work done, the universe will send you what you need.

—TONI CADE BAMBARA

All men should strive to learn before they die what they are running from, and to, and why.

—JAMES THURBER

Don't give up on you, 'cause when everyone's gone, you is all you got!

—A. R. BERNARD

More from God's Word

Above all and before all, do this: Get Wisdom! Write this at the top of your list: Get Understanding!

—PROVERBS 4:7 MSG

Wisdom is a tree of life to those who embrace her; happy are those who hold her tightly.

—PROVERBS 3:18 NLT

A Simple Step

If you can't accept yourself as you are, then you shouldn't really expect other people to accept you, either. But if you learn to accept yourself—to accept your weak points as well as your strong points—then you'll gain acceptance from the people who really matter, which, by the way, includes the person in the mirror.

Your Thoughts

35

Happiness Is . . .
Integrity

The man of integrity walks securely, but he who takes crooked paths will be found out.

—PROVERBS 10:9 NIV

If you'd like a surefire formula for making yourself unhappy, here's how you do it: Sow the seeds of deception wherever you go. But if you'd rather be happy, then you must guard your integrity like Uncle Sam guards Fort Knox.

It has been said that character is what we are when nobody is watching. How true. But there's never really a time when nobody is watching because God is always around, and He's always paying attention. As Bill Hybels observed, "Every secret act of character, conviction, and courage has been observed in living color by our omniscient God." Yes, God sees all; He knows all—and all of us should behave accordingly.

Are you willing to guard your words and watch your steps?

If so, you'll discover that living a life of integrity isn't always the easiest way, but it is always the right way.

So if you find yourself tempted to break the truth—or even to bend it—remember that honesty is God's policy . . . and it must also be yours. Simply put, if you really want to walk happily with God—and if you really want to guard your heart against the dangers of sin—you must protect your integrity at all costs. When you do, your character will take care of itself . . . and you won't need to look over your shoulder to see who, besides God, is watching.

Great Ideas About Integrity

Honesty is the first chapter in the book of wisdom.

    —THOMAS JEFFERSON

If the rascals knew the advantages of virtue, they would become honest.

    —BEN FRANKLIN

The most exhausting thing in life is being insincere.

    —ANNE MORROW LINDBERGH

Make your deeds follow your words. Keep your actions in line with your values. Keep your commitments to self and to others, and speak truth.

    —STEPHEN COVEY

Maintaining your integrity in a world of sham is no small accomplishment.

—WAYNE OATES

Integrity is the cornerstone of character. Honesty is the core of integrity.

—EDWIN LOUIS COLE

Decisions are not made at a particular moment of time; they are rooted in a man's character.

—A. R. BERNARD

More from God's Word

Good people will be guided by honesty; dishonesty will destroy those who are not trustworthy.

—PROVERBS 11:3 NCV

Innocent people will be kept safe, but those who are dishonest will suddenly be ruined.

—PROVERBS 28:18 NCV

A Simple Step

When telling the truth is hard, that probably means that you're afraid of what others might think—or what they might do—when you're truthful. Remember that it is usually better to face those kinds of problems now rather than later!

Your Thoughts

36

Happiness Is . . .
Being Involved in the Right Church for You

The church, you see, is not peripheral to the world; the world is peripheral to the church. The church is Christ's body, in which he speaks and acts, by which he fills everything with his presence.

—EPHESIANS 1:23 MSG

One of the most meaningful places to find happiness is within the four walls of your local church. And that's certainly not surprising, since the Bible teaches that we should worship God in our hearts and in our churches (Acts 20:28). We have clear instructions to "feed the church of God" and to worship our Creator in the presence of fellow believers, and that's precisely what we should do.

We live in a world that is teeming with temptations and distractions—a world where good and evil struggle in a constant battle to win our minds, our hearts, and our souls. Our

challenge, of course, is to ensure that we cast our lot on the side of God. One way that we remain faithful to Him is through the practice of regular, purposeful worship. When we worship the Father faithfully and fervently, we are blessed.

Are you an active member of your own fellowship? Are you a builder of bridges inside the four walls of your church and outside it? Do you contribute to God's glory by contributing your time and your talents to a close-knit band of believers? I hope so. The fellowship of believers is intended to be a powerful tool for spreading God's Good News and uplifting His children. God intends for you to be a fully contributing member of that fellowship. Your intentions should be the same.

Great Ideas About Church

The church needs people who are doers of the Word and not just hearers.

—WARREN WIERSBE

Churches do not lack great scholars and great minds. They lack men and women who can and will be channels of the power of God.

—CORRIE TEN BOOM

The church is not a museum for saints but a hospital for sinners.

—MORTON KELSEY

Only participation in the full life of a local church builds spiritual muscle.

—RICK WARREN

Don't ever come to church without coming as though it were the first time, as though it could be the best time, and as though it might be the last time.

—VANCE HAVNER

What a wonderful place to remind me that God is in control of my life. Church!

—A. R. BERNARD

More from God's Word

For where two or three are gathered together in My name, I am there among them.

—MATTHEW 18:20 HCSB

Be on guard for yourselves and for all the flock, among whom the Holy Spirit has appointed you as overseers, to shepherd the church of God, which He purchased with His own blood.

—ACTS 20:28 HCSB

A Simple Step

Make church a celebration, not an obligation. Your attitude toward church is important, in part, because it is contagious . . . so celebrate accordingly!

Your Thoughts

37

Happiness Is . . .
Maintaining Good Health

*And so, dear brothers and sisters, I plead with you to give your
bodies to God because of all he has done for you. Let them be a
living and holy sacrifice—the kind he will find acceptable. This is
truly the way to worship him.*

—ROMANS 12:1 NLT

ace facts: It's harder to be happy if you're not healthy.
Perhaps that's one of the reasons (but certainly not the
only reason) that the Bible teaches us to treat our bodies with care.

How do you treat your body? Do you treat it with the rever-
ence and respect it deserves, or do you take it more or less for
granted? Well, the Bible has clear instructions about the way
you should take care of the miraculous body that God has given
you. God's Word teaches us that our bodies are "temples" that
belong to God (1 Corinthians 6:19–20). We are commanded (not

encouraged, not advised—we are commanded!) to treat our bodies with respect and honor. We do so by making wise choices and by making those choices consistently over an extended period of time.

Do you sincerely seek to improve the overall quality of your life and your health? And would you like to experience the benefits of good health? Then promise yourself—and God—that you will begin making the kind of wise choices that will lead to a longer, healthier, happier life. The responsibility for those choices is yours. And so are the rewards.

Great Ideas About the Body

The first wealth is health.

—RALPH WALDO EMERSON

Look to your health; and if you have it, praise God and value it next to conscience; for health is the second blessing that we mortals are capable of, a blessing money can't buy.

—IZAAK WALTON

Mind and body in harmony provide all the necessary strength for happy, healthy living.

—CHARMAINE SAUNDERS

The body wants to be healthy. This is the natural condition. . . . When the body is out of balance, it wants to get back to it.

—ANDREW WEIL

Make a commitment to health and well-being, and develop a belief in the possibility of total health. Develop your own healing program, drawing on the support and advice of experts without becoming enslaved to them.

—BERNIE SIEGEL

Every man is the temple of God and the dwelling place of His Spirit. But His Spirit will not dwell in an unkempt temple.

—A. R. BERNARD

More from God's Word

Is any among you afflicted? Let him pray.

—JAMES 5:13 KJV

But I discipline my body and bring it into subjection, lest, when I have preached to others, I myself should become disqualified.

—1 CORINTHIANS 9:27 NKJV

Know ye not that ye are the temple of God and the Spirit of God dwelleth in you?

—1 CORINTHIANS 3:16 KJV

Beloved, I wish above all things that thou mayest prosper and be in health, even as thy soul prospereth.

—3 JOHN 2 KJV

A Simple Step

Remember: Life is a gift—health must be earned. We earn good health by cultivating healthy habits and by attending to our medical needs sooner rather than later (Ephesians 4:1).

Your Thoughts

38

Happiness Is . . .
Learning How to Deal with Difficult People

Bad temper is contagious—don't get infected.

—PROVERBS 22:25 MSG

L earning the art of happiness means learning how to deal with difficult people. After all, even the most saintly among us can be difficult to deal with at times. So it's inevitable that, from time to time, you'll encounter folks who behave inappropriately in the same way, or worse.

If you have occasion to deal with difficult people, remember the following tips:

1. Make Sure That You're Not the One Being Difficult: Perhaps the problems that concern you have their origin, at least partially, within your own heart. If so, fix yourself first (Philippians 2:3).

2. Don't Lecture: Lectures inevitably devolve into nagging;

nagging creates animosity, not lasting change. Since nagging usually creates more problems than it solves, save your breath (Proverbs 15:1).

3. Don't Become Caught Up in the Other Person's Emotional Outbursts: If someone is ranting, raving, or worse, you have the right to get up and leave. Remember: Emotions are highly contagious, so if the other person is angry, you will soon become angry, too. Instead of adding your own emotional energy to the outburst, you should make the conscious effort to remain calm—and part of remaining calm may be leaving the scene of the argument (Proverbs 22:24–25).

4. Stand Up for Yourself: If you're being mistreated, either physically, emotionally, or professionally, it's time to start taking care of yourself. But remember that standing up for yourself doesn't require an angry outburst on your part. You can (and probably should) stand up for yourself in a calm, mature, resolute manner. And you should do so sooner rather than later (Psalm 27:1).

5. Be Quick to Forgive: If you can't find it in your heart to forgive those who have hurt you, you're hurting yourself more than you're hurting anyone else.

Great Ideas About Difficult People

We are all fallen creatures and all very hard to live with.

—C. S. LEWIS

No one can make you jealous, angry, vengeful, or greedy . . .
unless you let him.

—NAPOLEON HILL

You are justified in avoiding people who send you from their
presence with less hope and strength to cope with life's
problems than when you met them.

—ELLA WHEELER WILCOX

A keen sense of humor helps us to overlook the unbecoming,
understand the unconventional, tolerate the unpleasant,
overcome the unexpected, and outlast the unbearable.

—BILLY GRAHAM

Judge your neighbor by his best moments, not his worst.

—FULTON J. SHEEN

More from God's Word

A contrary man spreads conflict, and a gossip separates
friends.

—PROVERBS 16:28 HCSB

Don't make friends with an angry man, and don't be a
companion of a hot-tempered man, or you will learn his ways
and entangle yourself in a snare.

—PROVERBS 22:24-25 HCSB

A Simple Step

Insist upon logical consequences to irresponsible behavior.
When you protect other people from the consequences of their
misbehavior, you're doing those folks a profound disservice. Most
people don't learn new behaviors until the old behaviors stop
working, so don't be an enabler (Hebrews 12:5-6).

Your Thoughts

39

Happiness Is . . .
Learning to Accept Change

*There is a time for everything, and a season for every activity
under heaven.*

—ECCLESIASTES 3:1 NIV

If you want to be happy, you'll need to learn how to roll with the punches. After all, this old world is in a state of constant change and so are we. At times, everything around us seems to be changing: Our children are growing up, we are growing older, loved ones pass on. Sometimes, the world seems to be trembling beneath our feet. But we can be comforted in the knowledge that our Heavenly Father is the rock that cannot be shaken. His Word promises, "I am the Lord, I do not change" (Malachi 3:6 NKJV).

Are you facing difficult transitions or unwelcome adjustments? If so, please remember that God is far bigger than any challenge you may face. So, instead of worrying about the shifting sands of life, put your faith in the One who cannot be moved.

Are you anxious about situations that you cannot control? Take your anxieties to God. Are you troubled? Take your troubles to Him. Does your world seem to be changing too fast for its own good? Remember that "Jesus Christ is the same yesterday, today, and forever" (Hebrews 13:8 NKJV). And, rest assured: It is precisely because your Creator does not change that you can face the transitions of life with courage for today and hope for tomorrow.

Great Ideas About Change

The secret of a happy life: Accept change gracefully.

—JIMMY STEWART

The horizon leans forward, offering you space to place new steps of change.

—MAYA ANGELOU

We are not retreating—we are advancing in another direction.

—DOUGLAS MACARTHUR

Always be in a state of becoming.

—WALT DISNEY

In a time of drastic change, it is the learners who inherit the future.

—ERIC HOFFER

Change is the essence of maturation. You won't mature unless
you are willing to change.

—A. R. BERNARD

More from God's Word

The prudent see danger and take refuge, but the simple keep
going and suffer from it.

—PROVERBS 27:12 NIV

Therefore do not worry about tomorrow, for tomorrow will worry
about itself. Each day has enough trouble of its own.

—MATTHEW 6:34 NIV

A Simple Step

If a big change is called for . . . don't be afraid to make it happen—
sometimes, one big leap is better than a thousand baby steps.

Your Thoughts

40

Happiness Is . . .
Genuine Enthusiasm for Life

*Whatever you do, do it enthusiastically, as something done for
the Lord and not for men.*

—COLOSSIANS 3:23 HCSB

Happiness and enthusiasm are traveling companions. The more enthusiastic you are about life, the happier you'll be. But if you allow your enthusiasm to fall flat, you'll soon discover that happiness is elusive.

If your zest for life has waned, it is now time to redirect your efforts and recharge your spiritual batteries. And that means refocusing your priorities (by putting God first) and counting your blessings (instead of your troubles). Genuine, heartfelt, enthusiastic Christianity is contagious. If you enjoy a life-altering relationship with God, that relationship will have an impact on others—perhaps a profound one.

Do you see each day as a glorious opportunity to serve God

and to do His will? Are you constantly praising God for His gifts, and are you sharing His Good News with the world? And are you excited about the possibilities for service that God has placed before you, whether at home, at work, at church, or at school? If you can answer these questions with a resounding "Yes!" you will be blessed . . . and you will be happy.

Remember: You are the recipient of Christ's sacrificial love. Accept it enthusiastically and share it fervently. Jesus deserves your enthusiasm; the world deserves it; and you deserve the experience of sharing it.

Great Ideas About Enthusiasm

Each day, I look for a kernel of excitement.

—BARBARA JORDAN

No person who is enthusiastic about his work has anything to fear from life.

—SAM GOLDWYN

Man's mind is not a container to be filled but rather a fire to be kindled.

—DOROTHEA BRANDE

Flaming enthusiasm, backed by horse sense and persistence, is the quality that most frequently makes for success.

—DALE CARNEGIE

What is required is sight and insight—then you might add one more: excite.

—ROBERT FROST

Don't wait to be motivated by someone else. Light your own fire.

—A. R. BERNARD

More from God's Word

So, my dear brothers and sisters, be strong and immovable. Always work enthusiastically for the Lord, for you know that nothing you do for the Lord is ever useless.

—1 CORINTHIANS 15:58 NLT

Do your work with enthusiasm. Work as if you were serving the Lord, not as if you were serving only men and women.

—EPHESIANS 6:7 NCV

And David was greatly distressed; for the people spake of stoning him, because the soul of all the people was grieved, every man for his sons and for his daughters: but David enouraged himself in the Lord his God.

—1 SAMUEL 30:6 KJV

A Simple Step

Don't wait for enthusiasm to find you—go looking for it. Look at your life and your relationships as exciting adventures. Don't wait for life to spice itself; spice things up yourself.

Your Thoughts

41

Happiness Is . . .
Facing Down Failure

Even though good people may be bothered by trouble seven times,
they are never defeated.

—PROVERBS 24:16 NCV

If you want to be happy, consistently happy, you must learn how to deal with failure. Why? Because all of us face setbacks from time to time—those occasional failures are simply the price we pay for being dues-paying members of the human race.

Mary Pickford was "America's sweetheart" in the early days of motion pictures. And along with Charlie Chaplin, Douglas Fairbanks, and D. W. Griffith, she formed United Artists Corporation, a Hollywood powerhouse.

Miss Pickford had a simple yet powerful formula for success: She said, "This thing we call 'failure' is not falling down, but staying down." She might well have added that every time we get back up, we build character.

Life's occasional setbacks are simply the price that we must pay for our willingness to take risks as we follow our dreams. But even when we encounter bitter disappointments, we must never lose faith.

Hebrews 10:36 advises, "Patient endurance is what you need now, so you will continue to do God's will. Then you will receive all that he has promised" (NLT). These words remind us that when we persevere, we will eventually receive the rewards which God has promised us. What's required is perseverance, not perfection.

When we face hardships, God stands ready to protect us. Our responsibility, of course, is to ask Him for protection. When we call upon Him in heartfelt prayer, He will answer. In His own time and according to His own plan, He will do His part to heal us. We, of course, must do our part, too.

And, while we are waiting for God's plans to unfold and for His healing touch to restore us, we can be comforted in the knowledge that our Creator can overcome any obstacle, even if we cannot.

Great Ideas About Failure

In order to be successful, you need to understand the feeling of failure and how to deal with that feeling.

—PHIL JACKSON

You may encounter many defeats, but you must not be defeated. In fact, it may be necessary to encounter the defeats,

so you can know who you are, what you can rise from, how you can still come out of it.

—MAYA ANGELOU

You may be disappointed if you fail, but you are doomed if you don't try.

—BEVERLY SILLS

You can learn little from victory. You can learn everything from defeat.

—CHRISTY MATHEWSON

Never equate losing with failure.

—ARTHUR ASHE

More from God's Word

They won't be afraid of bad news; their hearts are steady because they trust the Lord.

—PSALM 112:7 NCV

I took my troubles to the Lord; I cried out to him, and he answered my prayer.

—PSALM 120:1 NLT

A Simple Step

Setbacks are inevitable—your response to them is optional. You can turn your stumbling blocks into stepping stones . . . and you should. Failure is the womb for success.

Your Thoughts

42

Happiness Is . . .
Not Being a Victim

Do everything readily and cheerfully—no bickering, no second-guessing allowed!

—PHILIPPIANS 2:14 MSG

appiness is a choice—it depends on how you interpret life. To be happy, you must learn to interpret the world and its events in a positive fashion. This means that you begin programming yourself to see the good in everything—no matter what happens, no matter what goes down. Then, when you find the good in every situation, you take that good, and you build upon it.

It's amazing how many people, especially those who portray themselves as "victims," conclude that the lives they're experiencing have been chosen for them. But they're mistaken. In truth, their lives—all of our lives—are composed of our choices . . . and we become servants to the choices we make.

Every life, including yours, is a tapestry of choices. And the quality of your life depends, to a surprising extent, on the quality of the choices you make.

Would you like to enjoy a life of abundance and significance? If so, you must make choices that are pleasing to God.

From the instant you wake up in the morning until the moment you nod off to sleep at night, you make lots of decisions: decisions about the things you do, decisions about the words you speak, and decisions about the thoughts you choose to think. Today and every day, it's up to you (and only you) to make wise choices, choices that enhance your life and build a stronger relationship with the Creator. After all, He deserves your best . . . and so do you.

Great Ideas About Blame

Sooner or later, if people are to be healed, they must learn that the entirety of one's adult life is a series of personal choices, decisions. If they can accept this totally, then they become free people. To the extent that they do not accept this, they will forever feel themselves victims.

—M. SCOTT PECK

Never bend your head. Always hold it high. Look the world straight in the eye.

—HELEN KELLER

We must exchange the philosophy of excuse—what I am is
beyond my control—for the philosophy of responsibility.

—BARBARA JORDAN

Life ultimately means taking the responsibility to find the right
answer to its problems and to fulfill the tasks which it constantly
sets for each individual.

—VIKTOR FRANKL

Assume responsibility for the quality of your own life.

—NORMAN COUSINS

More from God's Word

If you do nothing in a difficult time, your strength is limited.

—PROVERBS 24:10 HCSB

Be strong and courageous. Do not be terrified; do not be
discouraged, for the LORD your God will be with you wherever
you go.

—JOSHUA 1:9 NIV

A Simple Step

*Don't think of yourself as a victim. Think of yourself as a person
who needs to take action now—and think of yourself as a person
who can! It's not what happens to you in life. It's what you do
about it (James 1:22).*

Your Thoughts

43

Happiness Is . . .
The Right Kind of Fun

Young man, it's wonderful to be young! Enjoy every minute of it.
Do everything you want to do; take it all in. But remember that
you must give an account to God for everything you do.

—ECCLESIASTES 11:9 NLT

Happiness means learning how to have the right kind of fun, which means fun that is pleasing to God. Are you a person who takes time each day to really enjoy life? Hopefully so. After all, you are the recipient of a precious gift—the gift of life. And because God has seen fit to give you this gift, it is important for you to use it and to enjoy it. But sometimes, amid the inevitable pressures of everyday living, really enjoying life may seem almost impossible. It is not.

For most of us, fun is as much a function of attitude as it is a function of environment. So whether you're standing victorious atop one of life's mountains or trudging through one of life's val-

leys, enjoy yourself. You deserve to have fun today, and God wants you to have fun today. So what on earth are you waiting for?

Great Ideas About Fun

People who cannot find time for recreation are obliged sooner or later to find time for illness.

—JOHN WANAMAKER

Wealth is not his that has it, but his that enjoys it.

—BEN FRANKLIN

We must will to be happy, and we must work at it.

—ALAIN

Life really must have joy. It's supposed to be fun!

—BARBARA BUSH

We should all do what in the long run gives us joy, even if it is only picking grapes or sorting the laundry.

—E. B. WHITE

Life is long; don't run out of fun!

—A. R. BERNARD

More from God's Word

Let the hearts of those who seek the LORD rejoice. Look to the LORD and his strength; seek his face always.

—1 CHRONICLES 16:10–11 NIV

I will praise you, Lord, with all my heart. I will tell all the miracles
you have done. I will be happy because of you; God Most High, I
will sing praises to your name.

—PSALM 9:1-2 NCV

A Simple Step

*Every day should be a cause for celebration. By celebrating the
gift of life, you protect your heart from the dangers of pessimism,
regret, hopelessness, and bitterness.*

Your Thoughts

_____

_____

_____

_____

_____

_____

_____

_____

_____

_____

_____

_____

_____

_____

44

Happiness Is . . .
Overcoming Envy

For where envy and self-seeking exist, confusion and every evil thing are there.

—JAMES 3:16 NKJV

Happiness and envy are mutually exclusive. You can be envious, or you can be happy, but you can't be both envious and happy. So the choice is yours: You can choose one or the other, but you can't choose both.

St. Augustine noted, "Whoever possesses God is happy." So here's a simple suggestion that is guaranteed to bring you happiness: Fill your heart with God's love, God's promises, and God's Son . . . and when you do so, leave no room for envy, hatred, bitterness, or regret.

As the recipient of God's grace, you have every reason to celebrate life. After all, God has promised you the opportunity to receive His abundance and His joy—in fact, you have the opportunity to receive those gifts right now. But if you allow envy to gnaw away at the fabric of your soul, you'll find that joy remains elusive. So do yourself an enormous favor: Rather than succumbing to the sin of envy, focus on the marvelous things that God has done for you—starting with Christ's sacrifice. Thank the Giver of all good gifts, and keep thanking Him for the wonders of His love and the miracles of His creation.

So, if you want a simple, surefire formula for a happier, healthier life, here it is: Count your own blessings and let your neighbors count theirs. It's the godly way to live.

Great Ideas About Envy

Discontent dries up the soul.

—ELISABETH ELLIOT

When you worry about what you don't have, you won't be able to enjoy what you do have.

—CHARLES SWINDOLL

As a moth gnaws a garment, so doth envy consume a man.

—ST. JOHN CHRYSOSTOM

Never indulge in jealousy or envy. Those two destructive emotions will eat you alive.

—LORETTA YOUNG

You can't be envious and happy at the same time.

—FRANK TYGER

Breaking news! The Joneses just declared bankruptcy, so you don't have to keep up with them anymore.

—A. R. BERNARD

More from God's Word

Let us not become boastful, challenging one another, envying one another.

—GALATIANS 5:26 NASB

Stop being angry! Turn from your rage! Do not lose your temper—it only leads to harm.

—PSALM 37:8 NLT

A Simple Step

Feelings of envy rob you of happiness and peace. Why rob yourself?

Your Thoughts

45

Happiness Is . . .
Learning to Master Money

*The plans of the diligent certainly lead to profit, but anyone who
is reckless only becomes poor.*

—PROVERBS 21:5 HCSB

ountless books have been written about money—how
to make it and how to keep it. But if you're a Christian,
you probably already own at least one copy—and probably several copies—of the world's foremost guide to financial
security. That book is the Holy Bible. God's Word is not only
a roadmap to eternal life, but it is also an indispensable guide-
book for life here on earth. As such, the Bible has much to say
about your life, your faith, and your finances.

God's Word reminds us again and again that our Creator
expects us to lead disciplined lives. God doesn't reward laziness,
misbehavior, or apathy. To the contrary, He expects believers
to behave with dignity and discipline . . . but the world tempts

us to do otherwise. We live in a world in which leisure is glorified and indifference is often glamorized. But God has other plans. He did not create us for lives of mediocrity; He created us for far greater things.

Life's greatest rewards seldom fall into our laps; to the contrary, our greatest accomplishments (including our financial accomplishments) usually require lots of work, a heaping helping of common sense, and a double dose of self-discipline—which is perfectly fine with God. After all, He knows that we're up to the task.

God's Word can help you organize your financial affairs in such a way that you have less need to worry and more time to celebrate. If that sounds appealing, keep reading God's book and apply it to every aspect of your life, including the way that you handle money. When you do, God will smile upon you and your finances.

Great Ideas About Money

Money is a training ground for God to develop (and for us to discover) our trustworthiness.

—LARRY BURKETT

The habit of saving is itself an education; it fosters every virtue, teaches self-discipline, cultivates the sense of order, trains to forethought, and broadens the mind.

—T. T. MUNGER

Beware of little expenses. A small leak will sink a great ship.

—BEN FRANKLIN

Budgeting is telling your money where to go instead of wondering where it went.

—JOHN MAXWELL

Money is a terrible master but an excellent servant.

—P. T. BARNUM

Budget! Then you won't have more month left over at the end of your money!

—A. R. BERNARD

More from God's Word

A faithful man will abound with blessings, but he who makes haste to be rich will not go unpunished.

—PROVERBS 28:20 NASB

If your wealth increases, don't make it the center of your life.

—PSALM 62:10 NLT

A Simple Step

Put God where He belongs—first. Any relationship that doesn't honor God is a relationship that is destined for problems—and that includes your relationship with money. So spend (and save) accordingly.

Your Thoughts

46

Happiness Is . . .
Celebrating Life

Celebrate God all day, every day. I mean, revel in him!

—PHILIPPIANS 4:4 MSG

Your life is a cause for celebration. Are you celebrating? Are you excited about your work, your family, and your future, or are you trudging through each day, smiling a little but worrying a lot? The answer to these questions will determine the level of your emotional health and, more important, the level of your spiritual health.

The comforting words of Psalm 118:24 remind us of a profound yet simple truth: "This is the day which the LORD hath made" (KJV). And if we are wise, we will rejoice in God's marvelous creation.

Today, celebrate the life that God has given you. Put a smile on your face, kind words on your lips, and a song in your heart. Be generous with your praise and free with your encouragement. And then, when you have celebrated life to the full, invite your friends to do likewise. After all, this is God's day, and He has given us clear instructions for its use. We are commanded to rejoice and be glad. So, with no further delay, let the celebration begin.

Great Ideas About Celebration

All our life is a celebration for us; we are convinced, in fact, that God is always everywhere. We sing while we work . . . we pray while we carry out all life's other occupations.

—ST. CLEMENT OF ALEXANDRIA

God knows everything, He cares about everything, He can manage everything, and He loves us. Surely this is enough for a fullness of joy that is beyond words.

—HANNAH WHITALL SMITH

A joyful heart is like a sunshine of God's love, the hope of eternal happiness, a burning flame of God. And if we pray, we will become that sunshine of God's love—in our own home, the place where we live, and in the world at large.

—MOTHER TERESA

Joy is the simplest form of gratitude.

—KARL BARTH

 A. R. Bernard

To get the full value of joy, you have to have someone to divide it with.

—MARK TWAIN

You never get a second chance to spend today. Make every day a celebration of life.

—A. R. BERNARD

More from God's Word

Make me hear joy and gladness.

—PSALM 51:8 NKJV

Shout with joy to the Lord, all the earth! Worship the Lord with gladness. Come before him, singing with joy.

—PSALM 100:1-2 NLT

A Simple Step

God has given you the gift of life (here on earth) and the promise of eternal life (in heaven). Now, He wants you to celebrate those gifts.

Your Thoughts

47

Happiness Is . . .
Taking Time to Laugh

A joyful heart is good medicine, but a broken spirit dries up the bones.

—PROVERBS 17:22 NASB

Laughter is medicine for the soul, but sometimes, amid the stresses of the day, we forget to take our medicine. Instead of viewing our world with a mixture of optimism and humor, we allow worries and distractions to rob us of the joy that God intends for our lives.

So the next time you find yourself dwelling upon the negatives of life, refocus your attention to things positive. The next time you find yourself falling prey to the blight of pessimism, stop yourself and turn your thoughts around. And, if you see your glass as "half empty," rest assured that your spiritual vision is impaired. With God, your glass is never half empty. With God as your protector and Christ as your Savior, your glass is filled to the brim and overflowing . . . forever.

Today, as you go about your daily activities, approach life with a smile on your lips and hope in your heart. And laugh every chance you get. After all, God created laughter for a reason . . . and Father indeed knows best. So laugh!

Great Ideas About Laughter

You don't have to be happy to laugh. You become happy because you laugh.

—BARBARA JOHNSON

Always laugh when you can. It is cheap medicine.

—LORD BYRON

Laughter is an instant vacation!

—MILTON BERLE

You're in for a great deal of pain if you take yourself too seriously.

—PAUL NEWMAN

Give me a sense of humor, Lord, and something to laugh about.

—ST. THOMAS MORE

How did I raise six boys? A lot of laughing!

—KAREN BERNARD

More from God's Word

Pride lands you flat on your face; humility prepares you for honors.

—PROVERBS 29:23 MSG

Before his downfall a man's heart is proud, but humility comes before honor.

—PROVERBS 18:12 NIV

A miserable heart means a miserable life; a cheerful heart fills the day with song.

—PROVERBS 15:15 MSG

A Simple Step

Get the whole family involved: Laughter is the icing on the cake of family life, and everybody in your clan deserves a slice.

Your Thoughts

48

Happiness Is . . .
Giving and Receiving Encouragement

But encourage each other every day while it is "today." Help each other so none of you will become hardened because sin has tricked you.

—HEBREWS 3:13 NCV

This world can be a difficult place, a place where many of our friends and family members are troubled by the challenges of everyday life. And since we cannot always be certain who needs our help, we should strive to speak helpful words to all who cross our paths.

Genuine encouragement should never be confused with pity. God intends for His children to lead lives of abundance, joy, celebration, and praise—not lives of self-pity or regret. So we must guard ourselves against hosting (or joining) the "pity parties" that so often accompany difficult times. Instead, we must encourage each other to have faith—first in God and His only begotten Son—and then in our own abilities to use the talents God has given us for the furtherance of His kingdom and for the betterment of our own lives.

When you think about it, with God on your side you have every reason to be hopeful, and you have every reason to share your hopes with others. When you do, you will discover that hope, like other human emotions, is contagious. So do the world (and yourself) a favor: Look for the good in others and celebrate the good that you find. When you do, you'll be a powerful force of encouragement to your friends and family . . . and a worthy servant to your Creator.

Great Ideas About Encouragement

Encouragement is the oxygen of the soul.

—JOHN MAXWELL

A positive mind tunes in to other positive minds.

—NAPOLEON HILL

Don't bring negatives to my door.

—MAYA ANGELOU

Don't waste yourself in rejection, nor bark against the bad, but chant the beauty of the good.

—RALPH WALDO EMERSON

When someone does something good, applaud! You'll make two people feel good.

—SAMUEL GOLDWYN

More from God's Word

So then, let us aim for harmony in the church and try to build each other up.

—ROMANS 14:19 NLT

A word spoken at the right time is like golden apples on a silver tray.

—PROVERBS 25:11 HCSB

A Simple Step

Do you want to be successful and go far in life? Encourage others to do the same. You can't lift other people up without lifting yourself up, too.

Your Thoughts

49

Happiness Is . . .
Being Optimistic

For God has not given us a spirit of fear and timidity, but of power, love, and self-discipline.

—2 TIMOTHY 1:7 NLT

If you're overly worried by the inevitable ups and downs of life, God wants to have a little chat with you. After all, God has made promises to you that He intends to keep. And if your life has been transformed by God's only begotten Son, then you, as a recipient of God's grace, have every reason to live courageously.

Are you willing to trust God's plans for your life? Hopefully, you will trust Him completely. After all, the words of the Psalmist make it clear: "The ways of God are without fault. The Lord's words are pure. He is a shield to those who trust him" (Psalm 18:30 NCV).

Even when your challenges seem overwhelming, you can be comforted in the knowledge that God remains steadfast. So make this promise to yourself and keep it—vow to be an expectant, faith-filled believer. Think optimistically about your life, your profession, your family, your future, and your purpose for living. Trust your hopes, not your fears. Take time to celebrate God's glorious creation. And then, when you've filled your heart with hope and happiness, share your optimism with others. They'll be better for it, and so will you.

Great Ideas About Optimism

I am an optimist. It does not seem to be much use being anything else.

—WINSTON CHURCHILL

At least ten times every day, affirm this thought: "I expect the best and, with God's help, I will attain the best."

—NORMAN VINCENT PEALE

I am happy and content because I think I am.

—ALAIN

Find the good. It's all around you. Find it, showcase it, and you'll start believing in it.

—JESSE OWENS

Without faith, nothing is possible. With it, nothing is impossible.

—MARY MCLEOD BETHUNE

Consider the ant: It never stops trying to find a way around any obstacle.

—A. R. BERNARD

More from God's Word

Be of good courage, and He shall strengthen your heart, all ye that hope in the Lord.

—PSALM 31:24 KJV

But if we look forward to something we don't yet have, we must wait patiently and confidently.

—ROMANS 8:25 NLT

A Simple Step

Be a realistic optimist. You should strive to think realistically about the future, but you should never confuse realism with pessimism. Your attitude toward the future will help create your future, so you might as well put the self-fulfilling prophecy to work for you by being both a realist and an optimist. And remember that life is far too short to be a pessimist.

Your Thoughts

50

Happiness Is . . .
Sensing God's Presence

Be still, and know that I am God . . .

—PSALM 46:10 KJV

I f God is everywhere, why does He sometimes seem so far away? The answer to that question, of course, has nothing to do with God and everything to do with us.

When we begin each day on our knees, in praise and worship to Him, God often seems very near indeed. But, if we ignore God's presence or—worse yet—rebel against Him altogether, the world in which we live becomes a spiritual wasteland.

Are you tired, discouraged, or fearful? Be comforted because God is with you. Are you confused? Listen to the quiet voice of your Heavenly Father. Are you bitter? Talk with God and seek His guidance. Are you celebrating a great victory? Thank God and praise Him. He is the Giver of all things good.

In whatever condition you find yourself, wherever you are—whether you are happy or sad, victorious or vanquished, troubled or triumphant—celebrate God's presence. And be comforted. God is not just near. He is here.

Great Ideas About God's Presence

We need never shout across the spaces to an absent God. He is nearer than our own soul, closer than our most secret thoughts.

—A. W. TOZER

The Lord Jesus by His Holy Spirit is with me, and the knowledge of His presence dispels the darkness and allays any fears.

—BILL BRIGHT

The world, space, and all visible components reverberate with God's presence and demonstrate His mighty power.

—FRANKLIN GRAHAM

Let this be your chief object in prayer: to realize the presence of your Heavenly Father. Let your watchword be: Alone with God.

—ANDREW MURRAY

If you want to hear God's voice clearly and you are uncertain, then remain in His presence until He changes that uncertainty. Often, much can happen during this waiting for the Lord.

Sometimes, He changes pride into humility, doubt into faith and peace.

—CORRIE TEN BOOM

More from God's Word

Be strong and courageous! Do not tremble or be dismayed, for the Lord your God is with you wherever you go.

—JOSHUA 1:9 NASB

I am not alone, because the Father is with Me.

—JOHN 16:32 HCSB

A Simple Step

Having trouble hearing God? If so, slow yourself down, tune out the distractions, and listen carefully. God has important things to say; your task is to be still and listen.

Your Thoughts

51

Happiness Is . . .
Discovering Genuine Peace

*Peace I leave with you. My peace I give to you. I do not give to you
as the world gives. Your heart must not be troubled or fearful.*

—JOHN 14:27 HCSB

One aspect of spiritual health is the ability to partake in
the peace that only God can give. Are you willing to
accept God's peace? If you can genuinely answer that
question with a resounding yes, then you are richly blessed.
But if you have not yet discovered "the peace that passes all
understanding," today is a wonderful day to find it.

The beautiful words of John 14:27 give us hope: "Peace
I leave with you, my peace I give to you. . . ." Jesus offers us
peace, not as the world gives, but as He alone gives. We, as
believers, can accept His peace or ignore it.

When we accept the peace of Jesus Christ into our hearts,
our lives are transformed. And then, because we possess the

gift of peace, we can share that gift with family members, friends, and the world. If, on the other hand, we choose to ignore the gift of peace—for whatever reason—we simply cannot share what we do not possess.

Today, as a gift to yourself, to your family, and to your friends, make peace with the past by forgiving those who have harmed you. Then claim the inner peace that is your spiritual birthright: the peace of Jesus Christ. It is offered freely; it has been paid for in full; it is yours for the asking. So ask. And then share.

Great Ideas About Peace

To know God as He really is—in His essential nature and character—is to arrive at a citadel of peace that circumstances may storm, but can never capture.

—CATHERINE MARSHALL

That peace, which has been described and which believers enjoy, is a participation of the peace which their glorious Lord and Master himself enjoys.

—JONATHAN EDWARDS

The fruit of our placing all things in God's hands is the presence of His abiding peace in our hearts.

—HANNAH WHITALL SMITH

There may be no trumpet sound or loud applause when we make a right decision, just a calm sense of resolution and peace.

—GLORIA GAITHER

The better acquainted you become with God, the less tensions you feel and the more peace you possess.

—CHARLES ALLEN

Peace is the umpire for doing the will of God.

—EDWIN LOUIS COLE

More from God's Word

I am coming to you now. But I pray these things while I am still in the world so that these followers can have all of my joy in them.

—JOHN 17:13 NCV

I have told you these things so that in Me you may have peace. You will have suffering in this world. Be courageous! I have conquered the world.

—JOHN 16:33 HCSB

A Simple Step

Do you want to discover God's peace? Then do your best to live in the center of God's will. Peace occurs naturally when your values and activities are in agreement!

Your Thoughts

Happiness Is . . .
Walking with God's Son

For God so loved the world that He gave His only begotten Son, that whoever believes in Him should not perish but have eternal life.

—JOHN 3:16 NKJV

S ince He walked this earth more than two thousand years ago, Jesus has called upon people of every generation (and that includes you) to follow in His footsteps. And God's Word promises that when you follow in Christ's footsteps, you will experience abundance, happiness, and joy.

Who will you choose to walk with today? Will you walk with shortsighted people who honor the ways of the world, or will you walk with the Son of God? Jesus walks with you. Are you walking with Him? Hopefully, you will choose to walk with Him today and every day of your life.

God doesn't want you to have a run-of-the-mill, follow-the-crowd kind of existence. God wants you to be a "new creation" through Him. And that's exactly what you should want for yourself, too. God deserves your extreme enthusiasm; the world deserves it; and you deserve the experience of sharing it. So what, neighbor, are you waiting for?

Great Ideas About Jesus

Think of this—we may live together with Him here and now, a daily walking with Him who loved us and gave Himself for us.

—ELISABETH ELLIOT

To walk out of His will is to walk into nowhere.

—C. S. LEWIS

When we truly walk with God throughout our day, life slowly starts to fall into place.

BILL HYBELS

Being a Christian is more than just an instantaneous conversion; it is like a daily process whereby you grow to be more and more like Christ.

—BILLY GRAHAM

Happiness is the by-product of a life that is lived in the will of God. When we humbly serve others, walk in God's path of holiness, and do what He tells us, then we will enjoy happiness.

—WARREN WIERSBE

More from God's Word

Whoever is not willing to carry the cross and follow me is not worthy of me. Those who try to hold on to their lives will give up true life. Those who give up their lives for me will hold on to true life.

—MATTHEW 10:38–39 NCV

If anyone would come after me, he must deny himself and take up his cross and follow me.

—MARK 8:34 NIV

A Simple Step

You don't have to be perfect to follow in Christ's footsteps. Jesus doesn't expect your perfection—He expects your participation.

Your Thoughts

 In Conclusion

Persistence

I t was the night of our annual staff Christmas dinner. We had more than one thousand staff members, full-time and volunteers.

Every December, we come together to celebrate one another as my wife Karen and I express our appreciation for those who serve the ministry and our community. We also use this as an opportunity to acknowledge staff members who have exhibited outstanding service during the year.

The night was still early, as Karen and I were moving from table to table greeting and thanking everyone. A new staff member stopped me in the middle of the aisle and asked, "Pastor, if you could sum up the secret of your success in one word, what would it be?" I immediately said, "God." But the young man didn't let me off the hook that easily. He said, "I know that God is first, but what practical key to your success can you give me in one word?"

I told him to give me a little time to think it through. No one had ever asked me a question like that. I wrestled with the question and finally one word came to mind—it was the word "persistence."

My thoughts turned back to a morning when I had listened to Pastor Chuck Swindoll as he quoted President Calvin Coolidge: Let me share Coolidge's words with you as I close this book.

PERSISTENCE

Nothing in the world can take the place of persistence.

Talent will not.

Nothing is more common than unsuccessful men with talent.

Genius will not.

Unrewarded genius is almost a proverb.

Education will not.

The world is full of educated derelicts.

Persistence and determination alone are omnipotent!

MY PRAYER

That you will discover that true meaning and happiness in life begins with a relationship with God!

Have a Happy Life!
A. R. Bernard

Permissions

The quoted ideas expressed in this book (but not scripture verses) are not, in all cases, exact quotations, as some have been edited for clarity and brevity. In all cases, the author has attempted to maintain the speaker's original intent. In some cases, quoted material for this book was obtained from secondary sources, primarily print media. While every effort was made to ensure the accuracy of these sources, the accuracy cannot be guaranteed. For additions, deletions, corrections, or clarifications in future editions of this text, please write A. R. Bernard Enterprises LLC.

Scripture quotations are taken from:

The Holy Bible, King James Version (KJV).

The Holy Bible, New International Version (NIV) Copyright © 1973, 1978, 1984, by International Bible Society. Used by permission of Zondervan Publishing House. All rights reserved.

The New American Standard Bible®, (NASB) Copyright © 1960, 1962, 1963, 1968, 1971, 1972, 1973, 1975, 1977, 1995 by The Lockman Foundation. Used by permission.

The Holy Bible, New King James Version (NKJV) Copyright © 1982 by Thomas Nelson, Inc. Used by permission

The Holy Bible, New Living Translation, (NLT) Copyright © 1996. Used by permission of Tyndale House Publishers, Inc., Wheaton, Illinois 60189. All rights reserved.

New Century Version®. (NCV) Copyright © 1987, 1988, 1991 by Word Publishing, a division of Thomas Nelson, Inc. All rights reserved. Used by permission.